I0796066

FAMILY THAI

BRINGING THE FLAVORS OF THAILAND HOME

ARNOLD MYINT
AND KAT THOMPSON

PHOTOGRAPHS BY LINDA XIAO

ABRAMS, NEW YORK

SALEM · WINSTON

When asked how she ended up in Nashville,
my mom would joke, "I wanted to be a country music star."
And though she may not have a Grammy to her name, she
definitely won the hearts of many in her community.

My mother's original self-published bifold cookbook was small and scrappy and devoted to teaching the Nashville community she fed and loved since 1975. In the introduction, she wrote, "This cookbook does not contain all the Thai dishes; there are more yet to come in future books." Cut to now, this book is in honor of my mother—a continuation of her groundwork and a dedication to her legacy.

TABLE OF CONTENTS

BOOT CAMP
LEMONADE 55 ¢

INTRODUCTION

Family Thais Run Deep

In 1984, my mother was pregnant with my sister. After long days at the restaurant, I remember her lying in bed with a spiral-bound notebook, writing recipes and taping small photocopied graphics onto the lined pages. She was creating a cookbook, her love letter to the customers.

Today, as the sun rises, before the bustle of the day, I'm cradling my daughter, Henley, in her nursery with my cell phone in hand, thumb feverishly typing this introduction to my own cookbook, which I see as my tribute to the food story my mother dedicated to her community many decades ago. It's come full circle.

International Market & Restaurant opened its doors in 1975, the first of its kind for Nashville, Tennessee. My mother and father, Thai and Burmese immigrants respectively, wanted to bring a slice of their culture to the Music City and introduce Americans to the fiery, bold, and fragrant flavors most comforting to them.

It made sense; back in Thailand, my mom and her family of nine siblings sold curries and stews on the street, eating whatever was left over at the end of a tiring and busy day. It might not have been much, but even then, she was an entrepreneur and brought that spirit, hunger, and know-how to her restaurant in America. What was a mode of survival for her eventually became a passion for me.

The family restaurant was open for two years before my arrival. It subsequently became everything to me: a makeshift castle, where I could traverse mountains made of stacked jasmine rice sacks; a workspace for doing homework; and the perfect place to throw a birthday party, year after year.

Whether I was working the till, serving customers scoops of curry and rice, peering at my grandma's nimble fingers as she folded dumpling after dumpling, or cajoling the aunties in the kitchen to teach me how to make a new dish (or at the very least, feed me), there have always been two constants in my life: family and food.

For my parents, Patti and Win Myint, there was no greater joy than breaking bread—or rice—in the restaurant and feeding an audience of new Thai food enthusiasts. Food is a love language in Thai. When Thais greet each other, we don't say, "How are you?" or "What's up?" Instead, we always ask, "Kin lao yang?" or "Have you eaten?" Sharing food with people from all walks of life was the way my parents showed their love.

In its more than fifty-year history, International Market has fed generations of people, hosted first dates that eventually turned into marriages and families, and was a fundamental stepping stone to the diverse food scene that Nashville has become today. My parents were pioneers, diving into the unknown headfirst and coming out on the other side, helping to transform Nashville into a more inclusive, welcoming, and interesting city. Although it wasn't always easy, they were adaptive and stayed focused on their vision for International Market.

With all of this in mind, it seems predestined that I would become a chef, right? But funnily enough, for the majority of my upbringing, I didn't think cooking would be a big part of my future.

Originally, I thought I'd become a performer. I came out of the womb flamboyant and colorful—I was never the cookie cutter Asian son. That didn't matter to my family. They always fully embraced me, and my interests were nourished and encouraged. I signed up for everything: Boy Scouts, camping, fishing, ice skating. I was a misfit on a mission to find my life's purpose. I wanted to get away from Nashville, to discover who I could become outside the confines of my hometown. I moved to New York City.

At first, I pursued figure skating. I loved the exhilaration I got from each competition and the opportunity to perform and connect with the music, costumes, and choreography. I felt like myself on the ice: fierce and beautiful and me. That being said, making a living as a figure skater is difficult. The sport can be isolating and a pro career short-lived.

When I decided to step away from the ice, I became interested in musical theater and acting. It was all the fun of performing in skating competitions without the sharp blades, frigid floors, and demoralizing scorecards.

But like every single person who has tried to make it as an actor in New York City, I experienced plenty of hurdles. I was simultaneously acting and working shifts in restaurants, unconsciously gravitating back to a world that reminded me of my childhood. It might seem bizarre, but the choreographed dance of dinner service was familiar to me, a comfort in a place that can be notoriously difficult for dreamers.

It was there in New York City, between auditions and restaurant shifts, that I realized nothing provided me as much joy and comfort as food—cooking it, smelling it, the tastes, the intensity, the clang of pans and buzz of dinner service, the camaraderie of a kitchen. Most of all, I loved witnessing the amazement and nourishment that the ritual of dining could provide others.

I decided to attend culinary school at the Institute of Culinary Education in New York City. I was having the time of my life bar-hopping and experiencing the city that never sleeps, so I figured why not continue this grand and wonderful journey? My parents never wavered in their support of me. For my dad, who was in education, getting a degree was the foundation for a real career, so he encouraged my decision to go to school.

Although I already had some foundational knowledge that I'd absorbed from my parents and aunties at International Market, culinary school was the place where I homed in on technique. To be honest, I was a bit of a brat—I thought I knew everything there was to know about food from my experiences in our restaurant. But the technique I acquired in school has been imperative to all my successes. It was here I was able to delight my teachers with the vibrancy of Thai flavors while pinning down the technical skills they taught me. I graduated in 2004 and then briefly taught at my alma mater's Los Angeles campus. I also worked for Jean-Georges Vongerichten, a chef who is an inspiration to me and who I wrote my first paper on while in culinary school. He once cooked in the royal palace of Thailand, and his marriage of Thai flavors with French technique resonated with me.

I'd go on to compete in season 7 of *Top Chef* and season 11 of *Food Network Star*, opportunities that felt like ideal intersections of my interests: There was the thrill of performance that had drawn me to acting and competition reminiscent of my skating days, and at the center of it all was food. I felt honored that I was being given a platform to represent my Asian and queer identity to a larger audience, and I've never wavered in my determination to celebrate this spicy, magical, and vibrant piece of my culture.

It's funny to look back at myself and my life experiences: I was a confused and lost kid running from home, seeking a different life, only to go all the way around the world and land back in Nashville, across the street from where the original International Market once stood. The second version of International Market, which I operate with my sister, Anna, continues to be a nod to my parents but also a way for me to connect with a new generation of IM fans and craft my own specialties.

When the pandemic struck and business slowed, I took the stay-at-home order as an opportunity to connect with Thai food enthusiasts beyond Nashville's borders and the limiting screens of reality television cooking shows. In 2020, I began using Instagram as a platform for culinary education and informative cooking videos. I talk about Thai ingredients, share recipes for some of my nostalgic favorites, and remix Thai dishes into something entirely new (like my version of pad see eiw that can use pappardelle instead of flat rice noodles; see page 135, where I teach you how to make it both ways). My follower count has jumped, and now I speak to a broad, global audience. It's a privilege to create content that Thai Americans can see themselves in, unapologetically showcase my queerness, and cultivate a greater appreciation for Thailand's food traditions.

Food, whether I'm indulging in it through the refined culinary experiences I've been fortunate enough to have or just sitting down to a casual family meal with my staff, is nourishment, culture, and memories wrapped up into one. Cooking Thai food is a way of seeing the world through my mom's eyes and is now a creative outlet for me to express myself—all while having fun and keeping my ancestors' recipes alive.

Working on this cookbook became not only a means for me to better understand myself as a Thai American, but also functions as a method of wading through grief and healing. I could not have written this book without my mom. For this reason, this cookbook is a culmination of my mom's legacy—a timestamp of who I was when my mom raised me and of the foods she fed me, and a community, to help us grow. Although she is no longer here physically, I feel her presence every time I cook and remain connected to her through our shared recipes and stories.

This cookbook is also a journey of self-discovery, establishing myself as a chef and combining my own techniques and flair for flavor—all while continuing to honor my mom. In these pages, I dive deep into must-have pantry staples for every home chef aspiring to cook Thai food, reveal how to prepare essentials like rice noodles and sticky rice, and devote a section to my family meal favorites. Longtime fans of International Market who have been begging for my mom's recipes for years will find some among these pages. I'll also share adaptations of Thai cuisine I've dreamt up myself, inspired by my hometown of Nashville and my travels around the world.

Whether you're a pro when it comes to Thai food and looking for a weekend project to attempt, or have only ever enjoyed Thai cuisine through takeout, this cookbook has something for all of you. There are more challenging techniques to attempt—like scratch-made tapioca dumplings and freshly steamed noodles—and easy riffs on classic Thai favorites, like my pounded green bean salad. I'll show you step-by-step techniques for folding dumplings and share my take on Thai culture through essays scattered throughout these pages. I've written this book not only for International Market enthusiasts but for everyone who has an interest in developing their skills as a home cook and wants to try their hand at Thai food.

This book is an embodiment of who I am: a Southern gay Thai American shaped by my family, experiences, the restaurant I grew up in, and my lifelong culinary pursuits. I want to show everyone how approachable and fun cooking not just Thai food, but *my* food, can really be.

Coca
355ml

My Way or the Thai Way

Authenticity can be a loaded term. The designation "authentic" has been used to both decry restaurants and celebrate them. It can be a force for good as well as a weapon to disparage. I have no problem with authenticity as a philosophy, but I don't like how it can be wielded to discredit restaurants. I'll explain what I mean.

When Thai food began gaining traction and popularity in the United States, it seemed like a set of rules appeared as to what made a restaurant authentic or not. Who came up with these rules? It's unclear. Sometimes, it's fellow Thai people who feel there is only one way to prepare Thai food. Other times, it's foreigners, known as *farang* in Thai, who have lived or vacationed in Thailand and think that because of their experiences, they are authorities on the cuisine.

I'm not saying that I have any authority over what constitutes "real" or "authentic" Thai food either. Yes, I may be Thai, but I was born and raised in America and, like many of you, I am just a genuine fan of the cuisine. The rules that some people use to dictate what is true Thai food, to me, have always seemed unfair or just plain inaccurate. Some examples: Thai restaurants that serve chow mein or orange chicken are inauthentic (this ignores the fact that Thai restaurant operators once had to adapt their menus to appeal to wider audiences); you can only use flat and wide rice noodles to make drunken noodles or pad see eiw (this is just untrue); and Thai food cannot be vegan because fish sauce is required for it to taste authentic (this ignores the rich history of plant-based Buddhist cuisine in Thailand).

As a restaurant kid who grew up in the eighties and witnessed almost every iteration of International Market, I'm here to say that everything my mom did, she did with authenticity. So, yeah, she used ketchup in pad Thai and named a dish she invented "Siam Chicken." She took traditionally Southern dishes, like braised cabbage, and put a Thai spin on them by incorporating ingredients like red curry paste and tofu. Whatever she did, my mom was fully and authentically herself: a Thai immigrant in Nashville, making delicious food to feed her community.

I'm now doing the same. I'm cooking the way my forefathers and mothers did and using what they had access to. The thing about Thai food is that you don't just eat it—you experience its regions. In the mountains of Chiang Mai, you taste the fermentations, the stews, the herbs native to higher elevation. In the beach towns of southern Thailand, the flavors of fresh seafood and extra-hot curries are intended to wake up sleepy, rainy villages. I am not necessarily looking to deviate from classic Thai flavors, but I do want to celebrate the resources I have access to in Nashville, my own little region of Thailand. So instead of barramundi for steamed fish dressed in lime juice, I'll source trout. If I can't find green papaya, I'll swap in green beans. Instead of a generic minced pork, I'll use pork belly from heritage farms. There's nothing right or wrong about it; I am being authentic to me, a chef at the intersection of Thai and Southern cuisine.

I think people are getting more hip to the changing tides. In recent years, a majority of the nominees for the James Beard Awards in Nashville went to Asian chefs and/or restaurants. The Beard committee celebrated dumplings, Thai family meals, and Japanese chilled udon. There was not a biscuit or barbecue in sight—and I'm proud to be among my peers to show the world that Southern food *can* and does include an Asian sensibility—and there's nothing inauthentic about that.

ASIAN BEST
TOTOLE
Granulated Chicken Flavor Soup Base Mix
ASIAN BEST
MAESRI
RICE STICKS

Welcome to the building blocks of Thailand's exciting, multilayered flavors. I know for some, Thai ingredients can feel daunting, but don't worry, I'm here to walk you through it. And while some items might be unfamiliar to you, the good news is that once you have gathered a few key things, many of which last a long time and are affordable to buy or easy to make, this pantry will set you up for success in cooking out of this book.

Some ingredients used to be extremely challenging to find—trust me, my parents were cooking pad Thai with ketchup back in the seventies—but today we are lucky that with just a little effort almost every ingredient can be tracked down at a specialty market or online, if not at your regular grocery store. It will be so worth it to try to get your hands on these specific items. I travel all over the world, not just in metropolitan cities that have access to everything, and I never have a huge issue finding products. There's almost always a small Asian grocer somewhere if you let curiosity and an excitement to explore lead you. You also might want to think about reaching out to your local Thai restaurant to see if they'll sell you a bottle of whatever it is you need. I know I've never denied a sale to one of our patrons. Occasionally, there are acceptable alternatives, and I'll list them. But in other instances, substitutes won't do—and I'll let you know when that is as well. In addition, the majority of the dishes in this book can be made using the standard kitchen tools that you probably already own, but there are just a few special things that come in handy for Thai cooking that I suggest you consider investing in, which I'll also highlight in this section. Let's build your Thai kitchen!

A NOTE ON PHONETIC SPELLING

The Thai alphabet is quite different from English. It includes more complex tones that don't always translate easily. You'll notice that throughout the book I've occasionally spelled ingredients or recipes differently from what you may be used to seeing. For example, I write *laab* instead of *larb*, *pad see eiw* instead of *pad see ew*, and *tao jiew* instead of *tao chio* (in reference to the fermented bean sauce). I am writing in a way that I think will lead to the most accurate pronunciation of the dish or ingredient—but it might not always be the same way other Thais write it! (Basically, I'm sneaking in a bonus learn-to-speak-Thai class for you.) I just wanted to give everyone a heads-up that my phonetic spelling may differ from other versions on menus or when you're shopping for ingredients.

BAKING POWDER
GROUND THYME
Tumeric
GROUND CINNAMON
Fennel Seed
BREAD CRUMB
Sugar
Red Lime Stone
CHINA SPICY MUSTARD
Salt
Black Peppercorn
PAPRIK
DRIED
Thailand's Number 1
GOLDEN MOUNTAIN SEASONING SAUCE
tương gia vị
SRIRACHA (Medium)
Chili Sauce
P·R·E·M·I·U
SWEET SOY SAUC
HEALTHY BOY BRAND
MUSHROOM SOY SAUCE
NET WT : 21 FL.OZ.
SOYBEAN PASTE
DEK SOM BOON
NET WEIGHT : 28.57 OZ.
PAROS
PRODUCT OF THAILAND

BOTTLE SERVICE

SWEET SOY SAUCE

Sweet soy sauce is typically used for marinades in barbecue, braises, and noodles. It has a staining quality that's so necessary to get that enticing umber hue found in a lot of Thai dishes, like pad see eiw. My go-to is the Thai Chinese brand made in Thailand called Healthy Boy. If you can't find sweet soy sauce, you can easily make it by adding sugar to a regular unsweetened soy sauce, like Kikkoman, and reducing it down over low heat until it's thickened to a nappe consistency—where it coats the back of a spoon. It won't be the exact flavor, but if you're in a pinch, it will do the trick.

BLACK SOY SAUCE

Black soy sauce is like sweet soy sauce in that it also is intended for staining food and adding depth of flavor. The viscosity is the same, but it's not nearly as sweet. It's used more for slowly building flavors in stir-fries and noodles. I think of it as the Worcestershire sauce of Asia.

FISH SAUCE

Fish sauce is the backbone of Thai cuisine. It brings a punch of umami that can be both subtle and overt, depending on the type of fish sauce you use and how it's used. Thais love to use plain fish sauce with sliced chiles as a condiment for practically every dish, so make sure you get your hands on a good-quality sauce. Tiparos is a brand I've used since I was a kid, and I love it, but honestly, my tip is to find a fish sauce you like, pick it, and stick to it. Different fish sauces have varying levels of pungency, so once you learn the language of your favorite fish sauce, it's much easier to gauge how to use it. Three Crabs, Squid, and Red Boat are all popular options. Commit—don't be a fish sauce slut.

OYSTER SAUCE

The secret weapon behind great pad krapao (page 132) is just a touch of oyster sauce. This bottled nectar adds umami, a little bit of thickness, and gentle sweetness. Just be forewarned: In Thailand, many dishes that claim to be vegetarian often include this, and just know that this definitely has seafood in it. If you follow a plant-based diet, there are vegan versions, like Lee Kum Kee's mushroom-based oyster sauce.

SAUCE GAI (SWEET CHILE SAUCE)

More sweet than spicy, sweet chile sauce (sauce gai) is the go-to sweet chile sauce to pair with fried chicken, tofu, and egg rolls. Although I'll also be teaching you how to make this sauce on page 60, it doesn't hurt to have a bottle of it stored away.

SRIRACHA

I'm going to teach you how to make this famous chile sauce in this cookbook (page 60), but if you're not up for the task, feel free to pick up a bottle. The famed Vietnamese American red rooster brand is much more heat-forward and acidic than the standard Thai sriracha, which is mellower and sweeter. When it comes to Thai cooking, I'd recommend Shark Brand or Golden Mountain.

THAI SEASONING SAUCE

Thai seasoning sauce is my go-to finishing sauce for everything. At my restaurant when people ask for soy sauce, knowing what they're expecting, we have to say, "We don't have that; we have seasoning sauce." It's a much lighter sauce than your Kikkomans or La Choys, in both color and level of saltiness, but with a bolder flavor. It is especially great on eggs, and I also love that it's vegan, and some varieties are even gluten-free (though be sure to double-check the ingredients if you have dietary restrictions, as they vary brand by brand). Just know that a little dash goes a long way. Golden Mountain is the brand I use, and Maggi is a close alternative but much saltier.

THAO JIEW (FERMENTED SOYBEAN PASTE)

This soybean paste, known as *thao jiew* in Thai, is an underrated building block of Thai cuisine. I think of it as a miso paste for the Thai pantry; it's basically salt-cured soybeans that, once they're hit with some heat during the cooking process, explode with flavor. You'll find this in the iconic pink seafood noodle soup called *yen ta fo*, stirred into the dipping sauce for Thai-style Hainanese chicken rice (page 232), and in the ubiquitous wok-fried morning glory dish called *pad boong fai dang* (see my take made with Brussels sprouts on page 142). It's a punch of wonderfully salty flavor that can't really be replicated with other ingredients. I use the Pantai or Healthy Boy brand.

THIN SOY SAUCE

Thin soy sauce, as you might have guessed, is a less concentrated version of regular soy sauce. Although it's not quite as salty, it still has a pleasing umami flavor. You can use this for dumpling fillings and in my version of Hainanese chicken rice (page 232).

VINEGAR

Most Thai dishes must have some form of acid, typically either through white distilled vinegar or lime juice. White distilled vinegar is also the base of a pickled chile condiment that is found on most Thai restaurant tables.

CANS AND JARS

BAMBOO SHOOTS

The most important thing to note about this ingredient is that it requires proper cleaning and some prep time. Make sure you drain the bamboo shoots thoroughly and boil them to remove impurities and calm their funky flavor. I love sliced shoots in a dumpling mix, curry, or stir-fry. If it's the star of the dish, like Om Nawmai, my bamboo dip on page 78, I like selecting bamboo tips that I can shred and make presentable.

To prepare bamboo shoots: Fill a medium saucepan three-quarters full of water and bring to a boil over high heat. Add the bamboo shoots and cook to release their impurities, 15 to 30 minutes. Drain the bamboo shoots and then either slice or shred. The prepared bamboo shoots can be stored in an airtight container in the refrigerator for up to a week.

COCONUT CREAM

Coconut cream is different from coconut milk. It's much thicker and often sweeter than coconut milk. We'll be using coconut cream for creamy and sweet Thai desserts.

COCONUT MILK

For curries, desserts, and even sometimes marinades, you're going to need coconut milk. It's extremely important to stock up on cans from Thailand, like Chaokoh or Aroy-D, not only for extra unctuous coconut flavor, but also texture. Thai coconut milk generally has a much thicker consistency than coconut milks from elsewhere, which will affect how rich and creamy your dish is.

DRIED MUSHROOMS

I love having dried mushrooms available because they rehydrate so easily and add so much earthiness to a dish. I typically keep shiitake, wood ears, and snow fungus on hand. Feel free to grab any of your favorites.

FRIED GARLIC

Same as the fried shallots (see below), but garlic. The bonus of frying garlic yourself is the liquid gold that is the leftover garlic oil (see page 65), but it doesn't hurt to have a store-bought version on hand as well.

FRIED SHALLOTS

You can make fried shallots yourself (I'll teach you how on page 64!), but if frying feels too intimidating, you'll find jarred fried shallots at most any Asian grocery store.

GRASS JELLY

I love the cooling effects of grass jelly, which is made from the Chinese herb mesona (a member of the mint family). It has an herbaceous aroma and subtle sweetness that's reminiscent of brown sugar, and the texture is like a firmer version of Jell-O. As a kid, my grandma would serve grass jelly to me straight with a couple of ice cubes, and that was already a refreshing dessert. Here, we'll be using it in our ruam mitt, or mixed fruit and jellies dessert (page 246).

JACKFRUIT

Canned jackfruit is wonderful because who has the time to wrestle with the spiky outer layer of a fresh jackfruit? We'll be using the yellow, ripe pods of canned jackfruit and incorporating them into Thai sweets.

KRACHAI

Krachai (aka fingerroot) is also known as Chinese ginger and gives warm spice, similar to galangal. Though it does come as a dried powder, like you'd find in a spice rack, I prefer the brined version (the whole roots) in a jar, easily found in an Asian market. Or an adequate substitute would be cilantro roots, and this is the actual root, beyond the stem (like, literally, what was in the ground).

LONGAN IN SYRUP

I liken longan to a firmer version of lychee. It, like lychee, is fleshy and incredibly sweet. Canned longan will come in handy in the dessert chapter of this book.

LYCHEE IN SYRUP

Canned lychee will also be a part of the dessert chapter, specifically for my Thai fruit cocktail recipe (page 246). There's not much you have to do to use it, but if you'd like it less sweet, you can rinse the syrup off before adding it to the fruit cocktail mix. Lychees are also great in cocktails and savory dishes.

AROY-D
JACKFRUIT IN SYRUP
MAESRI
GREEN CURRY PASTE
MAE PLOY
COCONUT CREAM
NƯỚC CỐT DỪA
PICKLED KACHAI WHITE
WATER CHESTNUTS
wei-chuan
WATER CHESTNUTS
Chin Chin
GRASS JELLY
GELEE de l'HERBE
ASIAN BEST
BAMBOO SHOOTS
STRIPS IN WATER
Red Lime Stone
กะปิดีคลองโคน
SHRIMP
LIME STONE PASTE (WHITE)
AROY-D
PALM'S SEEDS
(ATTAP) IN HEAVY SYRUP
Chin Chin
GREEN AI-YU JELLY
AI-YU VERT GELEE
ASIAN BEST
JACKFRUIT
IN SYRUP
MÍT NGỌT
AROY-D
LONGAN IN SYRUP
CONCENTRATED
COOKING TAMARIND
CONCENTRATE DE TAMARINDO
NET WT 16 OZ (454g)
CHAOKOH
COCONUT GEL IN SYRUP
NATA DE COCO
MAESRI
CHILLI PASTE IN SOYBEAN OIL
(Namprik Pao)
MAESRI
GREEN CURRY PASTE
MAESRI
RED CURRY PASTE
PRESERVED RADISH

NAM PRIK PAO (ROASTED CHILE JAM)

Smoky, roasted Thai chile jam packs so much flavor into stir-fries, curries, and dips. Yes, I could make this from scratch, but buying a jar is an efficient, and honestly delicious, shortcut. This paste is not as sharp as red curry paste, nor as spicy, but instead has a smoky and sweet roasted profile; there's a large depth of flavor to it. We'll be using it quite a lot in this book, but try spreading it on a turkey club sandwich, which was my mom's favorite way of enjoying it.

NEUTRAL COOKING OIL

I call for sunflower oil, but you can use canola oil, avocado oil, vegetable oil—I don't mind. Just find an oil with a neutral flavor and a high smoke point and we'll be in business.

PICKLED MUSTARD GREENS

I wouldn't say these are necessarily a flavor builder when it comes to Thai cooking, but some dishes—like khao thom, or rice soup (page 188) and my mom's curry noodle soup (page 190)—feel incomplete without a side of pickled mustard greens. As you can imagine, these add a vinegary zing to a dish, but the mustard greens also maintain a nice crunch in the canning process. Pigeon brand is a Thai favorite; their mustard greens are wonderfully tart and salty and can even be tossed with dried shrimp and chiles for a side dish.

RED BEANS IN SYRUP

Something you'll soon learn about Thais, or you may already be aware of, is that we love beans in our desserts. Red beans in syrup can be added to ice cream sandwiches (page 258) and ruam mitt, a coconut milk dessert full of beans and jellies (page 246).

RED AND GREEN CURRY PASTE

Some Thai cooks frown at the thought of using canned or jarred curry paste, but based on the evolution of quality resources, I think it's a great shortcut. To expedite cooking times, I like to use a prepared curry paste. You can always adapt and spruce up store-bought curry paste with the addition of fresh chiles, fish sauce, and makrut lime leaves, so don't be afraid to use a can (I like the brand Maesri). If you're not using the entire can of curry paste, you can store it in the freezer. I like to freeze it in mini-ice cube trays so I can easily use just a bit; it keeps great and maintains its flavor.

SALTED PRESERVED CABBAGE

This is a flavor enhancer specifically for soups and stir-fries. I like to think of it as a shortcut to rich, umami flavor, especially for my rice soup (page 188) and coconut curry noodles (page 190). The ingredients are simple; it's just cabbage, salt, sugar, and a little bit of garlic preserved in a jar. A little goes a long way, as it's quite salty. You can typically find salted preserved cabbage at the Asian grocery store.

SHRIMP PASTE, AKA GRAPI

Shrimp paste, or grapi (sometimes Romanized as *kapi*) provides the necessary funk that's found in so many Thai dishes. It most famously stars in khao kluk grapi, or shrimp paste rice (page 227), but is also the backbone of many dips and curry pastes. Be cognizant of its potent effects and lingering smell, but also don't be afraid to use it. Think of it similarly to the anchovy paste that makes Caesar salad so good.

SWEET PRESERVED RADISH

Don't sleep on sweet preserved radish. It might not be the first thing you think of when it comes to Thai cooking, but I consider it a secret weapon. Most traditional pad Thais have this in it, chopped so small it seamlessly melts into the dish. It's basically salt-and-sugar-cured daikon; I like to think of it as a Thai hot dog relish. This is also commonly found in omelets, and I use it in my sakoo sai moo, or sakoo pork dumplings (page 104).

SWEET SHREDDED COCONUT

Thai desserts are so often coconut-based that having sweet shredded coconut on hand—to bolster the flavor of coconut milk and coconut cream—is wise.

TAMARIND CONCENTRATE

Sticky tamarind concentrate is incredibly tart and a wonderful shortcut to tediously cooking down and straining the pulp of tamarind pods. We'll be using tamarind concentrate for our tamarind sauce (page 58), peanut sauce (page 70), and shrimp and pineapple curry (page 172), to name a few dishes. If you're using tamarind from a pod, make sure to dilute with water, as the fresh tamarind will be extra sharp.

WATER CHESTNUTS

Yes, you can add water chestnuts to dumplings, stir-fries, and curries, but one of the most prominent uses for these crunchy canned delights will be in my dessert chapter (see page 244).

DRY GOODS

BASIL SEEDS

I love basil seeds because they bloom so quickly, and they are filled with nourishing fiber. They are like a larger version of chia seeds. Basil seeds are commonly found in sweetened soy milk for breakfast in Thailand; they have a gooey texture almost like caviar. In Thai, they're referred to as "frog eggs" because that's what they resemble. We'll be using them as a garnish for our dessert sticky rice (page 242).

BEAN THREADS/GLASS NOODLES

Known as woon cent in Thai, bean threads, or glass noodles, are translucent noodles derived from mung beans. They're chewy—almost like the texture of jellyfish—and pretty flavorless, so they work well when absorbing tons of sauces, like in my mom's recipe for pad woon cent with pickled garlic (page 166). Make sure you're buying Thai-style glass noodles and not the Korean-style glass noodles made from sweet potato.

BROWN RICE

If you prefer the nuttiness of brown rice over jasmine rice, you can certainly swap in brown rice in any of my recipes for an added hit of fiber. I particularly enjoy serving brown rice with curries because it soaks up the broth so nicely while still maintaining its toothsome bite.

CORNSTARCH

If you ever find that a sauce you're preparing is too runny, make sure you have cornstarch on hand to make a slurry that will thicken the whole thing up (just mix equal parts water and starch). The same goes for some of the Thai desserts we'll be making; cornstarch adds body to dishes that may otherwise feel too watery. It also provides crunch to my Hat Yai fried chicken (page 235) and is a necessary component to dumpling skins and fresh noodles to ensure they don't stick.

DRIED EGG NOODLES

I have a recipe for making your own egg noodles from scratch in this book (page 44), but if you're not up for it, store-bought ones are great, too. Egg noodles are the perfect base for my Tofu Dang (page 114).

DRIED RICE NOODLES

The thing many people don't realize about Thailand is that the noodles are extremely customizable. Often when ordering wok noodles or noodle soup dishes in Thailand, it's common to be asked what size noodle you prefer. Although you might think thick rice noodles, known as *cent yai* in Thai, are mandatory for pad see eiw, you can use thin, angel hair–style rice noodles, also called *cent mee* in Thai, or pad Thai–style stick noodles (*cent lek*) on the packaging (or even deep-fried egg noodles) instead. The same goes for noodle soups at a noodle soup stall—you typically get to pick which type of noodle you want. My recipes give guidance on which noodles are more traditional for certain dishes, but feel free to remix if you want. Keep in mind that fresh rice noodles need to be separated before use, lest you end up with a clumpy noodle dish. Dry rice noodles, on the other hand, need to be soaked and boiled.

GINGKO NUTS

Gingko nuts have a buttery texture like beans and come from the gingko tree (those gorgeous trees that have leaves that resemble fans). I like the canned versions because they're already cleaned and pre-shelled so they're ready to use, but you can also make them yourself (see page 246). They are a common addition to Thai desserts. We'll be incorporating these plump seeds in a Thai-style fruit cocktail (see page 246).

JASMINE LONG-GRAIN RICE

This is one of Thailand's largest exports and the scent of my childhood. Jasmine long-grain rice has such an inviting aroma that pairs perfectly with curries, soups, spicy dips, salads—pretty much every Thai dish. No meal in Thailand is complete without it. Make sure you rinse the rice until the water runs clear before you cook it, to clean it and minimize the starch.

LIMESTONE

Limestone is a secret weapon in Thai cooking for adding an extra crispness to desserts like khanom buang (mini Thai crispy crepes) and my lotus cookies (page 248). It's almost like a sourdough starter; you'll want to add some water to the limestone powder and let it sit for at least 6 hours before incorporating it into a batter.

RICEBERRY RICE
PREMIUM QUALITY
ASIAN BEST
RED CARGO RICE
ASIAN BEST
RICE FLOUR
MAMA
WAI WAI
MAMA
ASIAN BEST
RICE STICKS
SIZE S
NON GMO
ASIAN BEST
TAPIOCA STARCH
ASIAN BEST
RICE STICKS
NON GMO
O-Cha
ASIAN BEST
MUNG BEAN
綠豆
ĐẬU XANH
ARGO
CORN STARCH
FOODSERVICE
NET WT 16 OZ (1 LB) 454 g
ASIAN BEST
STICKS
GLUTEN FREE
PRODUCT OF THAILAND
SIZE XL
TAPIOCA PEARLS
ASIAN BEST
PEELED SPLIT MUNG BEAN
NON GMO
ĐẬU XANH
MAMA
Oriental Style Instant Noodles
ARTIFICIAL PORK FLAVOR

MAMA THAI INSTANT RAMEN

In Thailand, Mama is practically the word for instant noodles like Kleenex is for tissues in America. Yes, it's a brand, but it's *the* brand. It's not uncommon to go to a Thai lunch spot and order zhuzhed up instant noodles for lunch. That's what we'll be doing here, too (page 202).

MUNG BEANS

Mung beans can be found in both savory and sweet applications in Thai cuisine, but for the sake of this book, we'll only be using them in desserts. This yellow bean adds a nuttiness to Thai sweets, but make sure you buy the versions that are already shelled (they should be yellow instead of green). You can soak mung beans and boil them to make mung bean pudding or roast them and use them as a crunchy topping. We'll be doing the latter for our fancy fruit with sticky rice (page 242).

RED RICE

Although very similar to brown rice in its cooking technique and flavor, red rice is slightly firmer and chewier. I love it for the toasted, nutty notes it gives off.

RICE FLOUR

Rice flour is added to meatballs, seafood fritters, the batter to prep rice noodles, and any other dish that needs some added bounce. It's different from glutinous rice flour, so make sure you grab the right version when shopping.

RICEBERRY RICE

Riceberry rice is a trendy, new Thai varietal (not to be mistaken for black rice). It cooks and eats more like farro or a hearty barley and is especially great as a cold salad.

STICKY RICE

Sticky rice, also known as glutinous rice or sweet rice, might seem intimidating to prepare, but it's quite easy, and I'll walk you through it (see page 38). Although it's labeled as sweet rice, these grains are not inherently sweet (though it is the base for sweet sticky rice desserts). The big thing to know is that sticky rice requires soaking time before you cook it, so it's an ingredient you need to plan for. Sticky rice is a common side dish for Northeastern Thai (or Isaan) dishes, so you'll want to prepare some to go with my pounded green bean salad (page 212) and jerky (page 110).

TAPIOCA PEARLS

We're going to be using tapioca pearls in both sweet and salty applications in this book. If you've ever had boba, this is a similar product—spherical and chewy balls made from tapioca—but much smaller. This is exactly like the tapioca you may have had in tapioca pudding. On the savory side, these are mandatory for my tapioca pork dumplings (page 104). On the sweet side, we'll be preparing a Thai take on tapioca pudding that's filled with corn kernels and sweet coconut cream.

TAPIOCA STARCH

Tapioca starch is required to make fresh rice noodles from scratch (see page 40), providing a level of bounciness that prepackaged noodles don't have. It also works great as a dry dredge for frying chicken and tofu.

VERMICELLI NOODLES

There are a couple different types of vermicelli noodles. One kind is thicker than an angel hair pasta and is made of fermented rice. In Thai, it's called *khanom jeen* and is sometimes marked as Vietnamese rice stick vermicelli on the packaging. This type of noodle is completely round, like spaghetti, rather than flat like fettucine or your standard pad Thai noodle. Often, if a packaged noodle is advertised as pad Thai stick noodles, that type of vermicelli will be flatter. Both noodles will work, it just depends on your preference. A good alternative if you can't find dried vermicelli noodles is Japanese somen wheat noodles. It's a component of my mom's signature lettuce wrap salad (page 218) and appears in curry broths. Lastly, angel hair vermicelli, known as *cent mee* in Thai, is a very thin, almost thread-like noodle that is used in stir-fry dishes, is an option for noodle soup, and fries up into the fun, puffy, crispy noodles used to garnish plates or make the crunchy snack called *mee krob*, where fried noodles are doused in a spicy or sweet sauce.

SUGARS AND SPICES

ASIAN CHICKEN BOUILLON (AKA MAGIC POWDER)

A small scoop of Asian chicken bouillon powder goes a long way in so many types of dishes—soups, meatballs, and even curries. It's not just salty; it's full-bodied umami that feels like a cooking hack to inject more eye-widening flavor in every bite. It's a shortcut to big flavor, which is why I call it Magic Powder. Knorr is the most popular brand, but there are alternative brands I like to use that are actually vegan, like Totole. I always have this on hand to take my dishes to the next level.

BROWN SUGAR

If you can't get your hands on palm sugar, brown sugar is the next best thing. I use brown sugar in my recipe for sriracha (page 60); the deep molasses flavor simmers beautifully with the vinegar and chiles.

CINNAMON

Cinnamon in Thai cooking is more associated with savory dishes than sweet. You'll typically find cinnamon where you'll also find star anise and five-spice—in soups and stews. Whole cinnamon sticks are very common and are used to infuse flavor into noodle broths, too.

CORIANDER SEEDS

It's amazing how tiny coriander seeds play such an important role in flavoring stocks and marinades. The flavor is a bit floral, reminiscent of sage, caraway, and perhaps a hint of citrus.

FIVE-SPICE POWDER

The five ingredients in this ground spice blend vary depending on the producer, but you'll typically find cinnamon, star anise, fennel seeds, cloves, and either white pepper, ginger, or Sichuan peppercorns. I think of five-spice as the baking or mulling spices of Thai food, offering a distinct warming component that gives a dish a cozy, more complex taste. It traditionally has been used to flavor savory dishes like braises, stews, and barbecue, but recently, it has been appearing in desserts, too. (I personally love tossing donuts in a blend of five-spice and sugar, like a Thai-style churro.)

GRANULATED SUGAR

If I don't specify the type of sugar in a recipe, then I am referring to classic granulated sugar. Sugar is in practically every Thai dish because you need a bit of sweetness to balance out the fish sauce, lime juice, and chiles. You'll use this for my fancy fruit and sticky rice (page 242) as well as in curries, salads, dips, and sauces.

KHAO KUAH (TOASTED RICE POWDER)

Toasted rice powder is exactly what it sounds like: grains of sticky rice are heated through until browned and then blitzed into a coarse powder. It is added to Thai salads like laab (page 210) for a nutty flavor and extra texture. You can find toasted rice powder in jars or plastic bags at Asian grocery stores, but I'll also teach you how to make it yourself (page 62).

KOSHER SALT

In all my recipes, whenever I mention salt, you can be confident that I'm talking about kosher salt. Kosher salt is less salty than table salt and is ideal for cooking because you can build levels of flavor as you cook. It's important to salt proteins before you start cooking them and then to continue to taste and salt as you go. Season your food!

MADRAS CURRY POWDER

There are a lot of Indian, Burmese, and Muslim influences in Thai cooking, and Madras curry powder is used in main dishes like noodles but also street snacks like satay and flaky curry puffs. This yellow curry powder contains a blend of spices and turmeric for color.

PALM SUGAR

Palm sugar is in practically every Thai dessert and is also used to sweeten savory dishes like curries. It's derived from toddy palm tree, where the sap is caramelized into a paste and often shaped into disks. To use the disks, simply shave off the amount of sugar you need for a recipe with a very sharp knife. Although you can use brown sugar as a substitute, it won't exactly match palm sugar's nutty notes.

PRIK POHN (TOASTED GROUND CHILE) AND WHOLE DRIED THAI CHILES

Thai dried chile flakes are very different from the Korean chile flakes gochugaru or the red pepper flakes you'd shake on pizza; they pack a walloping punch and are the reason behind the heat in many Thai dishes. These are made from dried Thai chiles, or bird's-eye chiles, which clock in on the Scoville scale at upward of 100,000 units (in comparison, jalapeños range between 2,000 and 8,000 units). You can make your own flakes at home (find instructions on page 54) simply by slow-roasting Thai chiles until dry in the oven and grinding them. We will cook with the whole dried chiles sometimes, too. Note that dried chiles will rehydrate and their spiciness will intensify while cooking. Use in moderation.

STAR ANISE

Star anise, usually a component in five-spice powder, gives a similar warm vibe as the spice blend, but I often use these cute star-shaped spices whole. They are ideal for long-simmered soups and stews, when there is time to gently infuse the cooking liquid with a comforting depth of flavor. These pods are tough, so I don't suggest eating them; you can discard them before serving or just avoid them.

TURMERIC

Turmeric not only adds a lovely golden color to the dishes, it also provides a faint pepperiness and mild sweetness. We'll be using turmeric in my version of chicken biryani (see page 128) and curry-based dishes.

WHITE PEPPER

If you follow me on social media, you know how much I love and celebrate white *pepperrrr*. It comes from the same pepper plant as black pepper but is picked at peak ripeness and has a mellower spiciness than black pepper. White pepper often is mixed with MSG, so when buying a shaker of this, please check the ingredients so you aren't oversalting your food in the cooking process. I like to think of white pepper as a creeping heat versus a forward heat like black pepper—white pepper is an alluring perfume, while black pepper is a more intense cologne. They're both great, but white pepper doesn't get stuck in your teeth!

FREEZER

DRIED SHRIMP

This is one of Thailand's most versatile ingredients. I use the water that I rehydrate dried shrimp in for stocks, coarsely grind them to use as a thickener and flavor booster in dishes like nam pla wahn (page 84) and my watermelon chile crumble (page 100), or leave them whole in dishes like papaya salad or sprinkled over rice porridge. It's umami, texture, and layers of flavor in one tiny ingredient. And they're pretty cute and fun to chew on!

DUMPLING WRAPPERS

You can make your own dumpling skins fresh (I teach you how on page 46), but for those moments when you don't want to prep and roll out your own dough, grab a pack of these and keep them in your freezer. You can find them in the freezer aisle of most Asian grocery stores.

FISH BALLS

Having fish balls on hand can lead to a fast, easy snack. I pop these in the air fryer and eat them with just a little sweet chile sauce. You'll find them in my curry vermicelli noodle dish (page 230). You can also add them to any soup or porridge.

FROZEN (STEAMED-CURED) MACKEREL

Salt-cured mackerel, otherwise known as pla tu, can last pretty much forever in the freezer. I always have some on hand to pan- or deep-fry and serve alongside my cha-om omelet and shrimp paste chile dip (page 74).

PROTEINS

I always have an assortment of proteins in my freezer—chicken thighs, fish fillets, steak, and pork shoulder (to name a few). Feel free to stock your freezer with whatever protein you like. Just make sure you properly wrap your proteins and store them in freezer-safe bags to ensure they don't get hit with freezer burn.

MEATBALLS

In addition to fish balls, I always keep my freezer stocked with pork and beef meatballs. The meatballs that contain bouncy bits of tendon are classic in Thai noodle soups and my favorite for a treat with some extra chew.

SATAW

If you have trouble sourcing fresh stink beans, also known as sataw (or sa-tor, as pictured), they can typically be found in the freezer section of an Asian grocery store. You'll need these fragrant beans for my punchy pad sataw recipe (page 144).

CHINESE-STYLE SAUSAGE

I love Chinese-style sausage, known as *gun chiang* in Thai. It's common to have this as a side dish with jhok or tossed into fried rice. Slice it up and cook it in a frying pan. A lot of fat tends to render from these sausages, so no oil is necessary.

ASIAN BEST
FRESH FROZEN
farm fresh
KAIZEN
FISH BALL
RUGBY SHAPE
NET WT 14 OZ (396g)
BANGKOK
BMC
MEATBALL CORP
BEEF AND
BEEF TENDON BALLS
A1128
牛筋丸
Bò Viên Gân
ASIAN BEST
CÁ BẠC MÁ HẤP
NET WT 9 OZ (256g)
KEEP FROZEN
WILD CAUGHT
ASIAN BEST
CÁ BẠC MÁ
清蒸鯖
BANGKOK
BMC
MEATBALL CORP
PORK M
豬肉丸
THỊT HEO VIÊN
SNAPPER
FILLETS
真味
HONG KONG STYLE DUMPLING WRAPPER
港式餃子皮
NET WT 14 OZ (396g)
白油腸
CHINESE STYLE CURED SAUSAGE
VENUS
全蛋銀絲麵
EGG NOODLE
LUCKY K.T. CO.

HANNAH

FRIDGE

BEAN SPROUTS

Bean sprouts add a delicious, vegetal crunch to my crispy mussel pancake (page 118). Make sure you thoroughly wash bean sprouts before using them because they sometimes have dirt or other mysterious residues on them.

BELL PEPPERS

Although bell peppers aren't as traditional, you'll often find them in Thai American restaurants to bulk up plates of pad krapao or curries. I love the volume they add to dishes and the subtle sweetness; feel free to incorporate them into stir-fries or curries.

CABBAGE

Cabbage is highly adaptable—we Thais often eat it raw, served as wedges to accompany particularly spicy dishes. It sweetens veggie-based soups as well and is also stellar simply stir-fried with a couple shakes of fish sauce. I also find shredded cabbage to be a great substitute when bean sprouts aren't easily accessible.

CARROTS

I love the versatility of carrots. I've found they are a great swap for papaya in papaya salads (an alternative I mention in my green bean som thum recipe on page 212). We'll also be using carrots to build broth and adding them to fried rice and my mom's famed pad macaroni (page 140).

CELERY

Celery provides a lovely crunch and a mildly sweet flavor (especially the leaves) to the salads in this cookbook. We'll also be using entire stalks of celery for making soup. Thai soups, like all great soups, benefit from a mirepoix of carrots, onion, and celery. Special bonus if you can find Chinese celery, which is a big slay thanks to its bolder, more peppery flavor.

CHINESE BROCCOLI

Every time I see a pad see eiw prepared with Western broccoli, I cry a little inside. These leafy and lengthy broccoli stems are mandatory for the wok-fired noodle dish; don't substitute the tree-shaped broccoli, which gets soggy in the wok almost immediately. Chinese broccoli is called *gai lan*, or *kannah*, in Thai.

CILANTRO

Cilantro is a key component of Thai soups and is often added to spicy sauces like jaeow (page 72) to lighten the heat. When most people think of cilantro, they think of the leaves. For Thais, however, the most desired part of cilantro is the root. Though you don't always find the whole plant in the grocery, if you come across cilantro roots at your farmers' market, use them; there is so much punchy, herbaceous flavor in those earthy tangles. The stems work almost as well, and the leaves are a common garnish. My mom taught me to never waste anything—so use the entirety of the herb when you have it! It's unfortunate that some people have a gene that makes cilantro taste soapy. If you are one of those poor souls, try substituting another herb, like Thai basil or even dill.

DAIKON RADISH

Daikon is a lot less sharp than our standard red radish. Its mild flavor is perfect to add to soups, where it becomes fork tender and is so comforting to eat. Make sure you peel it before you use it to create my perfect vegan broth (page 182).

DILL

Dill might not be an herb you think of when it comes to Thai cooking, but I honestly love it with Thai food so, so much. It is not necessarily traditional, but the grassiness of dill fits in perfectly with Thai salads.

EGGS

Stock up with at least a dozen eggs to cook through this cookbook! You'll need them for son-in-law eggs (page 102), steamed red curry fish custard (page 116), pad macaroni (page 140), as a topping for bacon pad krapao (page 132), and so much more.

FRESNO CHILES

I love Fresno chiles because they provide a kick of heat, but they also boast a captivating red color that makes dishes really pop when used as a garnish. We'll be using them to garnish a number of the dishes in the salad chapter.

GALANGAL

I need to begin by saying that galangal and ginger are two very different things, despite both being root spices. You cannot replace galangal with ginger. Galangal is used in curry pastes and soups like tom kha, a warm and comforting coconut broth soup that actually has galangal in the name (galangal is called *kha* in Thai). It has warm and spicy notes and a scent reminiscent of pine that adds so much depth to the dishes it touches. It comes in many forms: fresh, frozen, dried, and a dehydrated powder. Although fresh is preferred, any galangal you can get your hands on is better than substituting with ginger.

GARLIC

Garlic is the key to so many Thai dishes, whether it's the foundational flavor builder in the wok or just a garnish to complete a dish. It's the most forward note in my garlic pepper stir-fry (page 130), and I use at least six cloves for my Hat Yai fried chicken (page 235). You'll also find garlic in curries, soups, veggies, and rice dishes. Fried garlic (page 65) is a common finishing touch for fried chicken and porridges in Thailand, too, and is even enjoyed raw and pickled (see page 62). We'll be using a lot of garlic in this cookbook, so buckle up.

GINGER

You'll need grated and sliced ginger throughout this book for dips, curries, soups, and more. My tip is to throw a knob of the stuff in the freezer. It stays fresh, doesn't lose any of its potency, and you simply use a Microplane to grate it while still frozen when you need it. If you want to be more efficient, I'd suggest grinding the ginger down in a food processor and freezing it into cubes so you can have portioned ginger ready to go. Store fresh ginger root in a cool, dry place, like a fruit basket.

GREEN BEANS

Raw green beans are a common component of Thai crudité platters, chomped on raw with spicy dips like nam prik ong (page 80) and jaeow makuah (page 82). They're also the star of my som thum tua (page 212), a riff on papaya salad, so make sure to have some ready in your fridge.

LEMONGRASS

I love the smell of lemongrass. It's intoxicating and refreshing. Lemongrass is the key component to tom kha and tom yum soup, two spicy and bright soups that are popular in the Thai culinary canon. I also incorporate it into my om nawmai, or stewed bamboo shoot dip (page 78). Lemongrass can also be blitzed up in a food processor and added to marinades. Make sure to pound it to release its fragrance before adding. It's also excellent in a cocktail.

LIME

For spicy seafood sauce, steamed fish, papaya salad, and more, you're going to need lime. This citrus fruit does a lot of heavy lifting in the punchy flavors of Thai cooking, especially when paired with its equally important colleagues, garlic and Thai chiles. Limes are much more prevalent in Thai kitchens than lemons, which were once a rare, imported commodity. Fresh limes are best, as bottled juices sometimes have an acrid flavor. I love to cut them into cheeks (for instructions on how to do this, see page 50); this is a traditional Thai method, and it's much easier to extract juice when the lime is cut this way.

MAKRUT LIME LEAVES

The double leaves of the makrut lime tree have a citrusy aroma that can't really be replicated and are prominently featured in Thai cooking. The fruit isn't actually used, except maybe the rind, because it's quite bitter. But the leaves are fragrant and zesty; oddly enough, their flavor reminds me of Froot Loops. They are often cut into a chiffonade and sprinkled into curries, like my steamed red curry fish custard (page 116), and dips, like peanut sauce (page 70), or any dish that could benefit from a bright, floral finish.

MINT

Mint finds its way into a lot of Thai salads and wraps, like laab (page 210) and miang kham (my mom's iconic house salad wraps, page 218). It has a sweet fragrance that works well with other Thai ingredients, like shallots and lime. Don't add mint to really hot (in temperature) food, as it will wilt and blacken.

PANDAN

The aroma of fresh pandan leaves is intoxicating to me. It's earthy yet sweet like vanilla and subtle enough to be used in both savory and dessert applications. If you can find fresh pandan, the flavor will be much punchier and greener when blended and strained, but pandan extract is an efficient alternative. We'll primarily be using pandan in the desserts chapter of this cookbook, but you can also throw a knot of the stuff while steaming rice or even add it to water to make a perfumed drink.

PEANUTS

Peanuts are a common ingredient in Thai cooking. Find them in papaya salads, as a side dish to sour sausage, and even in curries. To release their nutty flavor, roast or heat them up in a sauté pan before use.

RED ONION

Red onions have a sweetness that white onions don't have, which makes thin slices of raw red onion a common garnish for Thai dishes. We'll also be cooking with red onion—find it in dips, my cucumber achaar salad (page 196), and my mom's salad (page 218).

SCALLIONS

Scallions, or green onions, provide a subtle allium flavor and can be used both raw as a garnish or cooked. I consider them my Western alternative to garlic chives (or guay chai). You'll find both the green and white parts of scallions throughout the recipes in this book, including the recipe for my grandmother's pork and shrimp shumai dumplings (page 92) and my red curry fried rice balls (page 98).

SERRANO CHILES

Although Thai chiles are the focal point of Thai cooking, I like mixing it up. Serranos aren't as spicy as Thai chiles and are particularly good for making the chile vinegar that's stocked in every Thai refrigerator (see the recipe on page 54).

SHALLOTS

I like to think of shallots as a cross between onions and garlic. They have so much flavor in such a small bulb—there's spice, there's sweet allium notes, there's bite. Shallots can be stir-fried as well as enjoyed raw in salads like laab and nam thok. Fried shallot is also a common topping in noodle and rice dishes.

THAI BASIL/HOLY BASIL

Not all basil is created equal. In Thai cooking, krapao—or holy basil—is the top dog. It has bite and so much fragrance. Another option, horapa, or Thai sweet basil, can sometimes be identified by its purple flowers and leaves and is usually easier to find at the grocery store. In my recipes, I simply call for Thai basil. Both versions work well, but Thai sweet basil is more mellow. If you can't find either of these two, tarragon is a great substitute. Just know it will not be the same; tarragon lacks the spicy, anise-forward flavor of holy basil. Many people use Italian basil instead, but I don't find it to be a good alternative because it tends to wilt and bruise easier than Thai varieties, leaving a muddled and bitter note. Try your best to get your hands on Thai sweet basil or holy basil if you can. (It's also easy to grow!)

THAI CHILES

Otherwise known as bird's-eye chiles, these red, green, orange, and yellow chiles are why people sometimes leave Thai restaurants sweating and crying—they're that hot. Some Thai grandmas chew on fresh Thai chiles as a snack. Although we probably won't be using them in that context (except for my mom's salad, page 218) in this cookbook, Thai chiles are essential for pretty much every Thai stir-fry dish and condiment. If it's a Thai dish with heat, it has Thai chiles. We often used them dried, too (see page 49 for more on these).

THAI EGGPLANT

Thai eggplant is a necessary component of my mom's eggplant curry (page 164) and also green curry. If you've ever eaten eggplant in Thai dishes before, you'll notice they're much smaller, rounder, and greener than the longer and purple-hued versions that are common stateside. These eggplants tend to be firmer than purple eggplants, so they hold up well in stir fries and curry dishes. Purple eggplants and the Japanese variety can be substituted (and are even used in my roasted eggplant dip on page 82), but the bitterness and texture of a Thai eggplant add so much depth that I'd encourage you to try to seek it out at the Asian grocery store when you can.

TOMATOES

Is there anything better than a summer tomato? Yes! Turning it into a savory tomato chile dip (page 80), adding tomato to fried rice (page 126), or incorporating it in a pounded salad. We'll be using tomatoes a lot here—I suggest cherry tomatoes for salad and Roma tomatoes for stir-fries.

TURKEY BERRY EGGPLANTS

Turkey berry eggplants are small and spherical, almost like tomatoes or grapes, with a bitter pop of flavor. Like the Thai eggplants above, you can substitute these with other kinds of eggplants that are easier to source, but they really heighten the dishes they're incorporated into, like my shrimp paste dip (page 74). And although I don't call for them in the recipe, they'd be a great addition to the green curry mussels (page 174) as well.

WHITE ONIONS

White onion is a bit more abrasive than red onion, so we won't be eating them raw very often. But have white onions ready to make soup stocks, stir-fry dishes, and dips.

SPECIAL EQUIPMENT

These are just a few specialized kitchen tools that you might not already own but will come in handy for cooking the recipes in this book.

BAMBOO STEAMER BASKET

This is a more versatile and accessible tool in the kitchen than the cone basket mentioned above. Not only can it achieve your sticky rice goals (with a flour sack towel, see below), it's also perfect for cooking dumplings, fresh noodles, vegetables, fish, etc. It comes in a variety of sizes and is easy to store.

COFFEE GRINDER

This is my alternative hack to a mortar and pestle when grinding spices. It's less time consuming—but keep a separate grinder for your coffee, as it is almost impossible to clean it enough to remove every trace of the bold flavors you are grinding.

FLOUR SACK TOWEL

When making sticky rice, a flour sack ensures the rice doesn't get stuck to the walls of the steaming basket. These are easy to find and work really well to line bamboo steamer baskets when making sticky rice, I actually love this way more than cheesecloth when it comes to other Thai recipe applications.

LARGE MORTAR AND PESTLE

The *krok*, or large mortar and pestle, is synonymous with achieving the perfect *thum* (a pounded Thai-style salad), northern Thai dips, and curry paste. It has been proven to extract more pronounced flavors from base ingredients than a food processor.

LARGE STOCKPOT (8 QUART / 7.6 L)

Every house needs one. But home cooks seldom own one. Now is your time! A large stockpot is great for soaking, marinating, boiling, frying, making soups, making stocks. Trust me, you'll use it a lot after you invest in it.

MASKING TAPE AND SHARPIE

This recommendation is my chef gift to you: Label and date your food. It's undoubtedly the most efficient way to stay organized and safe. FIFO! (First In, First Out.)

MULTIUSE KNIFE

Every chef needs a multifunctional knife, something sturdy enough to cut through bones and starchy root vegetables and sleek enough for finely mincing garlic and shallots.

THAI BRASS FLOWER MOLD WITH HANDLE

This mold exists for one specific purpose: For the Thai food enthusiast who wants to create the perfect lotus cookie (page 248), you'll be happy to know that with a quick web search, it can be in your mailbox in days.

ROLLING PIN

You'll need a rolling pin for rolling out dumpling skins or noodles, especially if you don't have a pasta machine. Any style of rolling pin—tapered, straight, handled—will do.

SPIDER

I don't know why I love this tool so much; it's probably one of the most underrated kitchen essentials. I use it for hard-cooked eggs, to strain small batches of pasta, when blanching vegetables, and even skimming fat. Spiders come in a variety of sizes, and you should stock all of them.

THAI STICKY RICE STEAM BASKET AND POT

This cone-shaped basket is the tool that is identified with the traditional Thai method of making sticky rice. This two-part set of basket and pot work in tandem to simply achieve the authentic flavor and texture we want, but don't worry, it's still possible to make good sticky rice without this—and I'll walk you through it on page 38.

TONGS

Whether grabbing something off a fiery grill or assembling a plate, I always have tongs on hand in my kitchen. I prefer metal tongs over silicone-tipped ones as they're grippier and I find them easier to maneuver, but use whatever you have in your kitchen.

Before we get to the elaborate braises, the tapioca pearl dumplings, and my fancy take on mango sticky rice, we have to begin with the basics. Rice and noodles are such a foundational part of Thai cuisine that if you don't know how to prepare these two carbs properly, you're setting yourself up for failure. Don't worry, though! I will show you step-by-step how to make everything, from baskets of sticky rice to freshly steamed noodles.

When it comes to preparing rice, everything is very measured; just make sure you use enough water and give yourself enough time to properly steam everything. And always wash your rice. I like to wash it until the water runs clear, usually two or three times. With noodles and dumpling skins, it's all about feel. Get your hands dirty when working that dough and be unafraid to try, fail, and try again. If you've ever made fresh pasta, you'll find my egg noodle recipe to be practically the same thing. It's good fun, and you'll be so proud when you can make dumplings and noodles from scratch. All your hard work is sure to lead to delicious results.

HOW TO COOK Rice

Makes 4 cups (560 g)

I couldn't get this far in this cookbook without talking about rice because, as you flip through the pages and recipes, you'll soon learn how important rice is to Thai food. Rice is the foundation of almost every Thai dish. I'm serious—even desserts. You can eat rice in soups, accompanying curries, with fried eggs, and even in Thai-style ice cream sundaes. Rice flour is used for frying, making sweet dumplings, preparing fresh noodles, or as a thickening agent.

We Thais take a lot of pride in our rolodex of rices, particularly our jasmine rice, which has a floral fragrance that's unlike any other variety out there. The long-grain shape of Thai rice makes it much less sticky than Japanese rice and it tends to be much fluffier when freshly steamed. The farmers in Thailand work hard to till the land and produce our rice, which also happens to be one of the largest exports of our country.

The smell of freshly steamed rice is one of my favorite scents. I swear, everyone comes running when they hear the rice cooker click with completion and a cloud of sweet rice aroma fills the air.

Although most Thais cook rice in a cooker, I know that not everyone has one at home. But that doesn't matter; you can achieve great rice on the stovetop, too. The important thing here is to wash your rice, and for sticky rice, soaking it goes a long way. Not only is it necessary to clean your rice (who knows where the rice has been!), but it's also important to release the excess starch so the grains don't stick together and turn gummy. Here's how I prepare rice with or without a cooker.

2 cups (390 g) jasmine long-grain rice

In a fine-mesh sieve, rinse the rice until the water runs clear. Place the rinsed rice in a rice cooker in an even layer, pour 2½ cups (600 ml) water over the rice, and press Cook following the manufacturer's instructions. Once the cooker alerts you that the rice is fully cooked, take a fork and fluff the rice. Keep it covered and leave the cooker set to warm until time for serving.

To cook rice on a stovetop, rinse the rice and place it in a medium saucepan. Add 2½ cups (600 ml) water and bring to a boil. Reduce the heat to maintain a simmer, cover the pot, and cook for 12 to 15 minutes, until the rice grains are fully cooked and all the water is absorbed. Fluff the rice with a fork and keep covered until ready to serve.

Store leftover cooked rice in an airtight container in the refrigerator for up to 4 days.

HOW TO MAKE Sticky Rice

Makes 2 cups (530 g)

My cardinal rule about sticky rice is this: You must eat it fresh. Sticky rice does not refrigerate or freeze well. It tends to clump up and harden, and microwaving it only dehydrates it further. I can instantly tell when a Thai restaurant does this hack of reheating sticky rice in small sandwich bags. Trust me, the result is not worth it (we do *not* do this at International Market—our kitchen doesn't even have a microwave). If you want to enjoy sticky rice, please, please steam it fresh. To steam sticky rice, I use a traditional Thai sticky rice steamer pot and bamboo basket. You can typically find these at Thai and Lao grocery stores, as well as online. The cone-shaped bamboo basket, which resembles a funnel, slots neatly into the aluminum pot, ensuring the steam rises evenly to cook the rice. Here's exactly how I prepare my sticky rice.

2 cups (400 g) sticky rice

In a fine-mesh sieve, rinse the rice until the water runs mostly clear. Place the rinsed rice in a medium bowl, cover with water, and let soak for at least 4 hours and up to 12 hours. Drain and set aside. In a large saucepot or stockpot, soak the traditional bamboo cone steam basket, if using, for 20 minutes. Drain and set aside.

Pour water to come 1 inch (2.5 cm) up the sides of the bamboo cone's aluminum steamer pot. Place over high heat and bring to a boil. Place the soaked bamboo cone steam basket (see Note) over the boiling water, making sure the water doesn't touch the base of the basket. Put the soaked rice into the basket, cover with a lid that fits the basket and covers the rice completely, and steam without stirring or lifting the lid until the rice grains are partially cooked, about 20 minutes. Remove the lid, lift the basket with both hands, and then flip the rice by lightly tossing the rice in the basket until it turns over. Return the basket to the pot, cover again, and continue to cook until the grains are bouncy (think gummy bear texture), 10 to 15 minutes longer. Remove the rice from the steam basket and serve warm or at room temperature.

Note: If using a stainless-steel or bamboo steamer basket instead of the cone, line the grates of the steamer with a soaked flour sack towel or thin cloth. Place the rice in the center and wrap the edges of the cloth over the top of the rice. Cover the pot and steam for 20 to 25 minutes, until bouncy.

SANPATONG
GLUTEN FREE

HOW TO MAKE Fresh Rice Noodles

Makes 2½ cups (13 ounces / 370 g) noodles (6 sheets)

Rice noodles are a blank canvas for delicious flavor. Large swaths of noodles, known as *kuay tiew cent yai*, are typically used in stir-fried dishes like pad see eiw and drunken noodles. Thinner noodles, or cent lek (aka small noodles), can be served up in noodle soups like kuay tiew tom yum or boat noodles. You can roll rice noodles into tight cylinders the size of Korean rice cakes to prepare kuay jub, a street food soup that's known for its fragrant and peppery broth.

Whatever you choose to use your rice noodles for, making them from scratch is not as intimidating as it might seem. During the pandemic, when it was difficult to get my hands on fresh rice noodles, this was my method for keeping International Market stocked and my cravings satisfied. Making fresh rice noodles is a flex that will impress any dinner party guest! And when you make them yourself, you can control the thickness and find your preferred texture (and even if some batches are wonkier than others, it adds character to a dish). All you need is some sort of steamer or a large braiser, a baking pan (even a brownie tin would work), and some self-confidence to turn this rice flour–based batter into delectably bouncy sheets of noodles that you can cut and customize to suit any recipe. And, hey—if your first batches need some work, you can always destroy the evidence by eating them. That's a win-win, if you ask me.

1 cup (105 g) Thai rice flour
⅓ cup (45 g) tapioca starch
1 teaspoon kosher salt
Nonstick cooking spray

Pour water into a saucepan large enough to fit a steamer basket to come 2 inches (2.5 cm) up the sides. Bring to a boil over high heat.

In a medium bowl, combine the rice flour, tapioca starch, and salt. Slowly add 1¼ cups (300 ml) water **(1)** and whisk until the batter is completely smooth and has the consistency of milk. Evenly spray a very light coat of oil onto a pie pan, brownie tin, or small baking pan that will fit into your steamer basket (ideally the noodles will be 6 to 8 inches / 15 to 20 cm long, depending on your pan) and use a pastry or silicone brush to brush out any bubbles.

Place the pan into the steamer basket and place the steamer basket over the saucepan. Pour 3 ounces (⅓ cup / 90 ml) of batter into the prepared pan **(2)** and evenly coat the bottom. Cover with the steamer lid and steam until the batter begins to bubble, about 4 minutes. Remove the pan with the batter and let it cool slightly. Carefully remove the noodle sheet **(3)**, using a rubber spatula if necessary, and transfer it to a cutting board. Cut the sheet into long noodles about ⅜ inch (1 cm) (slightly wider than fettuccine but not as wide as pappardelle) **(4)**. Repeat with the remaining batter.

If not using the noodles immediately, lightly coat them with cooking spray to prevent sticking and store them in an airtight container in the refrigerator for up to 3 days.

1
RICE

2

3

4

HOW TO WORK WITH Dry Rice Noodles

When you go to a Thai noodle stand, one of the first questions you'll be asked is, "What kind of noodles would you like?" There are angel hair–like strands, small noodles, wide flat sheets—all of which are made from the same rice noodle base, but provide a completely different textural dining experience.

The same type of variety can be found in dry noodles. Depending on what type of noodle you're after—small, large, or vermicelli—be sure to carefully examine the packaging to find the type you're looking for. Unlike other dry noodles, like pasta, you can't just boil dried rice noodles in water and call it a day, lest you want your noodles to be rendered into a clumpy mess. Although stocks and sauces are so important to noodle-based dishes, noodles are the star component, so you want to be careful to not overcook or undercook them.

Instead, stock up your pantry with this versatile ingredient and follow these instructions (the timing may vary depending on the size of noodles you end up using, so also be sure to consult the instructions on the package).

Soak dry rice noodles in warm water, completely submerged, for 15 to 30 minutes, depending on the thickness of the noodle. The noodles will rehydrate and become pliable, though they will not be fully cooked.

Remove the rehydrated noodles from the soaking water and store in an airtight container or zip-top bag for up to 3 days.

When it's time to cook the noodles, dip the desired portion into boiling water for 10 to 15 seconds, depending on the thickness of the noodle. Remove from the boiling water and add to your skillet or soup bowl.

HOW TO MAKE Ba Mee (Egg Noodles)

Makes about 10 ounces (280 g)

Egg noodles have a beautiful golden hue and bouncy texture that pairs well with my char siu tofu (page 114) or in wonton soup. When making egg noodles, think of it as making pasta; the dough needs to rest and the process may take some time, but the yellow strands that emerge from this endeavor are hard to beat. I recommend the thicker fettuccine setting for this recipe because it has a higher success rate for beginners. Once the dough is made and the noodles are cut, keep them refrigerated until you are ready to cook. The cook time is a mere 90 seconds; then toss them with garlic oil to prevent the noodles from sticking and pair them with your favorite protein or noodle soup.

- 1 large egg, at room temperature
- 1 large egg yolk, at room temperature
- 2 tablespoons neutral oil, such as sunflower
- 2 tablespoons warm water
- 1 cup (130 g) all-purpose flour, plus additional for kneading
- 3 tablespoons tapioca starch, plus additional for dusting the noodles
- 1 teaspoon kosher salt
- ½ teaspoon sugar

In a large liquid measuring cup, using a fork, whisk together the egg, egg yolk, oil, and warm water. Set aside.

In the bowl of a stand mixer fitted with the dough hook, combine the flour, tapioca starch, salt, and sugar. Beat on low speed until evenly combined, about 1 minute. Increase the speed to medium and slowly drizzle one-third of the liquid, letting the flour grab the liquid and gradually start to clump. Turn off the mixer and, with a rubber spatula, scrape the dough to the center of the bowl. Add the remaining liquid, half at a time, until a dough ball forms around the hook, and continue mixing until the dough is slightly sticky but easily releases from your fingers, about 2 minutes.

Lightly dust a dry work surface with flour. Turn the dough out onto the surface and knead it until smooth and elastic, 2 to 3 minutes, adding flour if it is too sticky. Shape the dough into a ball; wrap in plastic wrap and let rest for 15 minutes.

Divide the dough into 4 pieces. Using a rolling pin, roll each dough piece into a ¼-inch-thick (6 mm) oval to fit through a pasta machine. Keep the other pieces covered with plastic wrap while rolling to prevent them from drying out.

Using a pasta machine set to the thickest setting, roll one piece of dough through to make a thin pasta sheet. Fold the sheet like a letter and pass it through again. Lower the setting and pass through again, rolling and folding. Progressively lower the setting, rolling and folding, until you reach the fettuccine setting (5 on some machines, or about 2 away from the thinnest setting). Shape the noodles by using the fettuccine setting on the roller to cut the sheet into ¼-inch (6 mm) strips. Repeat with remaining pieces (see Note).

Once the noodles are cut, lightly toss in tapioca starch, then cover and refrigerate until ready to use. Store in an airtight container in the refrigerator for up to 3 days.

Note: If you don't have a pasta machine, use a rolling pin to roll a sheet to your desired thinness. Lightly dust the pasta sheet with flour, fold the sheet onto itself, and, using a knife, cut the sheet into ¼-inch (6 mm) strips.

HOW TO MAKE Dumpling Skins

Makes 48 skins

You *could* buy dumpling skins in the freezer section of an Asian grocery store, but what's the fun in that? Making them yourself requires a bit of finger dexterity to ensure you're rolling the skins out thinly and evenly, but when you do it yourself, you get to decide the shape and size of your dumplings.

- 1 teaspoon kosher salt
- 1 cup (240 ml) hot but not boiling water
- 2 cups (255 g) all-purpose flour, plus additional for kneading
- Cornstarch, if not using right away

In a medium bowl or large liquid measuring cup, dissolve the salt into the hot water. Put the flour in a large bowl and gradually add the salt-water mixture one-third at a time, mixing with your hands, until fully combined. The dough should feel firm, elastic, and not too wet.

On a very lightly floured work surface, knead the dough until it's soft and some of the moisture has been released, 3 to 5 minutes (be sure not to overwork the dough or it will crack when you're rolling it). Portion the dough into 4 pieces and roll each piece into a long tube the size of a hot dog (6 inches x 1 inch / 15 cm x 2.5 cm). You may want to wrap or keep the pieces covered with plastic while rolling to prevent them from drying out. Cut the tubes crosswise into ½-inch (12 mm) rounds. Roll each round into a ball and use a rolling pin to shape them into paper-thin (5-inch x 5-inch / 12 cm x 12 cm) round disks. Repeat with the remaining dough.

If you're making your skins in advance, dust cornstarch in between the layers to prevent the dough from getting too sticky and refrigerate in an airtight container for up to 4 days.

Some Like It Hot

There is a preconceived notion that all Thai food is spicy. I hear this in the restaurant all the time—will this be too spicy for me if I can't handle hot food? I know there are people who have been burned, literally, by Thai food before, but I also want to show that not every dish in Thailand's gastronomy is spicy.

For starters, there's a recipe in this cookbook for gaeng jeud (page 180), a dish whose name directly translates to "bland soup" in Thai. The soup, to me, isn't actually bland—it's full of the hearty flavors of simmered chicken bones and daikon radish. It is, however, incredibly simple, comforting, and, as you may have guessed, not spicy whatsoever. Gang jeud is a common accompaniment to khao mahn gai (page 232), Thailand's version of chicken fat rice. Although there are spicy sauces that can be paired with khao mahn gai, this dish, too, is not inherently spicy. At its core, it is poached chicken with rice steamed in chicken fat and stock.

Not every Thai person is born with a talent for crushing plates full of chiles or fiery curries. These palates are developed by our parents and grandparents, and sometimes not at all. You'd be amazed at the number of Thai people who don't like their food to be overly spicy or can't handle spice. Like any group of people, the experiences of the individuals within the Thai community are vast and different. Not loving spicy food does not make any one person any less Thai, just as chomping on raw chiles alongside sour green mango doesn't make anyone more Thai.

Spice is also subjective. What may feel spicy to me may not be as hot to you. It's why you see condiment caddies at almost every Thai restaurant in and out of Thailand. The condiment caddies—which traditionally hold sugar, fish sauce with chiles, chiles in vinegar, and coarsely ground dried chiles—allow customers to customize their food to their own tastes. In Thailand, there is no such thing as offending the chef by seasoning your dish. Some may like their noodle soup with the extra pickle flavor of chiles soaked in vinegar, while others prefer a pad see eiw with added sweetness. Some may like their yum mama with extra chiles, while others enjoy their meals as is. Whatever the case, our palates are all different.

In this cookbook, I give a guide for how spicy I typically like my dishes that have chiles in them, but this is just a reference point. If you know you like your pad krapao extra hot, by all means incorporate extra chiles! If you want your pounded green bean salad to be less spicy, use less. Spice levels are entirely subjective, but I'd describe my preference as a happy medium: hot enough to amplify flavor but not so spicy that it detracts from the dish. And if you're looking for dishes that aren't inherently spicy at all, there are plenty throughout this book in the form of my grandma's dumplings, egg rolls, beef jerky, and more.

HOW TO CUT Lime Cheeks

There are many ways to figure out if someone is Thai. Perhaps they text "555" instead of "hahaha" (Thailand's version of LOL, as the word *five* is pronounced "ha" in Thai), or shout "Oh ho!" when they're in disbelief. One surefire method, for me, is to spot how they cut limes.

Cutting limes into cheeks, instead of straight across a lime's equator, is a kitchen hack passed down from generation to generation in Thailand's culture. I don't know who discovered this method or when exactly it was implemented, but I know every Thai person does it like this—and for good reason! This is the most effective way to get juice out of your limes and ensure you're getting the most out of your citrus. It's incredibly easy, too: just follow these simple instructions. You'll never cut limes any other way again.

Hold the lime vertically on your cutting board and slice down one side, avoiding the core, to cut the first cheek **(1)**.

Rotate the lime by one-third and slice through again, avoiding the core, to remove the second cheek.

Rotate again and slice the remaining third, avoiding the core, for your final cheek **(2)**.

Note: Instead of merely using the lime juice for a salad, Thais tend to toss the whole lime cheek inside. This is not only to keep with tradition, but to add depth of flavor. Though inedible, the lime skin's oils and bitterness from the zest deepen and punctuate the brightness of the salad.

"Fen Fly"

Before we dive into my Thai snack favorites, I'd be remiss to not mention a dish that was my biggest takeaway from when I lived in Bangkok in my early twenties: French fries. It's true, these fried potato matchsticks transcended cultures, social classes, and were readily available at all hours of the day. Although ketchup and mayonnaise are universally beloved condiments for fries, Thais bring a next-level condiment game when it comes to fast food, pairing the crispy potatoes with sweet and sticky sauce gai (page 60) and punchy hot sauce.

Thai people love to season their food. It's not seen as offensive to ask a Thai chef for a condiment caddy—small glass jars holding sugar, chiles, fish sauce, and spicy vinegar—to load your noodle soup up with extra heat or give your pad see eiw an extra sprinkling of sweetness. In Thai, there's a phrase, *took leen*, which translates to "it's right for my tongue." Thais move through life knowing that every person's palate is different and it's okay to adapt your food to your specific likings. You'll likely see these condiment caddies on tables in Thai restaurants both in the US and in Thailand, but who says you can't also have these seasoning basics readily available in your home?

Most of the pantry items we're going to be preparing can be found and bought in grocery stores (and in Chapter 1, I share some of my favorite items to stock up on, see pages 17–31). But I'd be remiss if I didn't show you how to make them yourself from scratch. You'll be amazed at how simple it is to churn out prik nam som (chile vinegar, page 54), crispy fried shallots (page 64), and nutty toasted rice powder (page 62). If you've been saving the extra chile vinegar or chile powder packets from your local Thai takeout spot, you don't have to do that anymore because now you can make them yourself. Most of these flavor enhancers—from sauces to beloved crispy, fried garnishes—take mere minutes to prepare and last a long time in the fridge or pantry, so you can always have them on hand to boost the flavor of your food.

CONDIMENT CADDY

Prik Pohn
Toasted Ground Chile

Makes about 2 cups (165 g)

You can find this condiment in every Thai home. Although it's typically used to finish a dish or customize a bowl of noodles, sometimes toasted chile flakes are also used in cooking or to make a sauce. Preparing them is easy—in terms of tools, all you really need is an oven and a way to process the chiles. Back in the day, chiles were dried in the sun and then ground down using a mortar and pestle. Now we have ovens and food processors to speed up the process. Ultimately, it depends on how fine of a grind you'd like. The mortar and pestle method takes a lot more effort, but the payoff is large flakes of Thai chiles. The food processor might make a finer powder, but it requires way less energy. Whichever method you opt for, once you have prik pohn in your pantry, you'll never want to be without it.

6 ounces (170 g) dried Thai chiles (about 6 packed cups)

Preheat the oven to 250°F (120°C).

Spread the chiles evenly on a baking sheet. Toast until very fragrant and crisp, 15 to 25 minutes. (Alternatively, if you want to make a smaller batch, you can toast the chiles in a large skillet over low heat, tossing frequently, until fragrant, 4 to 6 minutes.) Remove from the heat and let cool.

In a mortar with a pestle, spice grinder, or food processor, grind the toasted chiles, in batches if necessary, until coarsely ground into small flakes.

Store in an airtight container (like a lidded glass jar) for up to 6 months.

Prik Nam Som
Chile Vinegar

Makes about 1½ cups (360 ml)

If you ever find a Thai dish needing a hit of tang, you can remedy that either with a squeeze of lime or a spoonful of prik nam som. *Prik nam som*, which translates to "chile vinegar," is exactly that. There are versions of this that are blended into a sauce and others that are just sliced chiles pickled in vinegar (this one is the latter). I've seen it prepared with jalapeños as well, but I like serranos because they have more heat. The best part of the recipe is that it takes less than five minutes to throw together—and just a bit of time to sit before it's ready for use (overnight is even better to truly let the flavors develop). When making this at home, I simply put all the ingredients in a jar and give it a shake. When scaling this recipe up at the restaurant, we dump everything in a vat and give it a stir. It couldn't be easier—and it will add so much finishing flair to your dishes that you'll always want to have a jar of this in your fridge.

1 tablespoon sugar
¼ teaspoon kosher salt
1 cup (240 ml) distilled white vinegar
6 large cloves garlic, thinly sliced
4 large serrano chiles, thinly sliced

In a 16-ounce (480 ml) lidded glass jar, combine the sugar, salt, and vinegar; cover and shake until the sugar is fully dissolved. Add the sliced garlic and serrano chiles, then cover and shake again to combine. Store in the refrigerator overnight. Serve at room temperature.

It will keep in the refrigerator for up to 1 week.

CLOCKWISE FROM TOP: Prik Nam Som (opposite), Prik Nam Pla (page 56), Prik Pohn (opposite)

Prik Nam Pla

Chile Fish Sauce

Makes about ⅓ cup (75 ml)

This is the lifeblood of Thailand. If you cut me open, I'd probably leak prik nam pla. The name directly translates to chile fish sauce, and that's essentially what this is—a sauce of fish sauce, chiles, a hit of sugar and lime, and some garlic. You'll find prik nam pla in every condiment caddy in Thailand right next to the sugar, dried chiles, and chile vinegar. Use it for fried eggs, noodles—pretty much everything goes.

- **3 tablespoons fish sauce**
- **2 tablespoons chopped fresh red Thai chiles (about 10 chiles)**
- **1 tablespoon minced garlic**
- **1 tablespoon fresh lime juice**
- **1 tablespoon sugar**

In an 8-ounce (240 ml) lidded glass jar, combine the fish sauce, Thai chiles, garlic, lime juice, and sugar and stir until the sugar is dissolved, about 2 minutes. Serve at room temperature.

Store in the refrigerator for up to 1 month.

Note: A condiment caddy pro tip from Arnold—although the condiment caddy is a choose-your-own-adventure, I don't always recommend every condiment for every dish. When I'm out at a Thai restaurant, these are the dishes I pair these condiments with.

Prik nam som: pad see eiw, raad nah (gravy noodles), or polloh (five-spice stew)

Prik nam pla: fried rice, Thai omelet, or pad krapao

Prik pohn: laab, pad Thai, or crying tiger salad

Sugar: Sugar is the final component in a condiment caddy, and although you don't need a recipe for it, you might want to know when to use it. In Thailand, we use it like salt and pepper—adjust to taste!

DIPPING SAUCES

Mom's Hot Sauce

Makes 2¾ cups (660 ml)

This hot sauce is extra-spicy and very vinegary and has been in my family since the first day I was in the restaurant. It's a star of my mom's condiment caddy. The only thing I can really compare it to is a very rustic, unstrained Tabasco. To this day, one touch of this sauce on the tip of my tongue reduces me to a hiccup fit. I'm amazed that customers douse their food with it, but I love that they appreciate it as much as I do. If you don't want to make it, you can pick up a bottle at International Market next time you're in the neighborhood.

- 1 ounce (30 g) dried Thai chiles (about ¾ packed cup)
- 1 ounce (30 g) dried arbol chiles (about 1 packed cup)
- 3 cups (720 ml) warm water
- 1½ teaspoons finely chopped garlic
- ½ teaspoon kosher salt
- ½ teaspoon sugar
- 2 cups (480 ml) distilled white vinegar

In a 32-ounce (960 ml) glass jar or large bowl, combine the Thai chiles and arbol chiles and cover with the warm water. Place a pickling weight or a sealed zip-top bag filled with enough water to submerge the chiles completely in the warm water on top. Cover lightly with plastic wrap and let stand at room temperature for 3 days to rehydrate.

Strain the chiles and transfer to a blender. Add the garlic, salt, sugar, and vinegar and blend on low speed until just combined. Use immediately or store in a lidded glass jar at room temperature for up to 2 weeks or in the refrigerator for up to 3 months.

International Market OG Sweet and Sour Sauce

Makes about 1 cup (240 ml)

Growing up, I was confused why this wasn't the sticky red stuff we typically got whenever we picked up Chinese takeout. To me, that was the definition of a sweet and sour sauce. My mom's riff, however, uses black soy sauce, so it was brown instead of bright red and had added umami. It was inspired by the Chinese sauce, especially because people expected every Asian restaurant to have a sweet and sour sauce, but it was made my mom's way. Despite being confused by the color, I never questioned my mom—customers seemed to love it, and I was always proud when people would ask for an additional side of this sauce. It's sweet and sour, as the name suggests, and it's incredibly easy to make, too. I love that a sauce with only four ingredients can come together into such a developed flavor.

- 1 cup (200 g) sugar
- ½ teaspoon kosher salt
- 1½ cups (360 ml) distilled white vinegar
- 1 teaspoon black soy sauce

In a medium saucepan, combine the sugar, salt, and vinegar and cook over medium heat until the liquid is reduced by half and the mixture is sticky like a syrup, about 20 minutes. Remove from the heat, whisk in the soy sauce, and let cool completely.

Use immediately or store in an airtight container (like a lidded glass jar) in the refrigerator for up to 3 months.

Dumpling Sauce

Makes 1 cup (240 ml)

This dumpling sauce is similar to the Chinese version you might pair with xiaolongbao or potstickers, but a tad sweeter thanks to the sweet soy sauce and with a bit more of a spicy and garlicky kick. If you've ever had my grandma's khanom jeeb (or dumplings) at International Market (page 92), this is the sauce that accompanies those perfect parcels.

- **¼ cup (60 ml) sweet soy sauce**
- **¼ cup (60 ml) black soy sauce**
- **¼ cup (60 ml) white distilled vinegar**
- **1 tablespoon finely chopped garlic**
- **1 tablespoon finely chopped, peeled fresh ginger**
- **½ teaspoon Prik Pohn (Toasted Ground Chile, page 54) or crushed dried Thai chile (about 1 chile)**

In a medium saucepan, combine the sweet soy sauce, black soy sauce, vinegar, garlic, ginger, prik pohn, and ¼ cup (60 ml) water and bring to a simmer over medium heat. Simmer until the garlic and ginger are tender and the liquid is fragrant, about 3 minutes. Remove from the heat and let cool.

Serve immediately or store in an airtight container (like a lidded glass jar) in the refrigerator for up to 2 weeks.

Tamarind Sauce

Makes 2¾ cups (660 ml)

This tamarind sauce is the base of pad Thai, but it's also the tangy sauce that accompanies my mom's legendary "house salad" (page 218), and what I pour over son-in-law eggs (page 102). It takes minutes to stir together; the result is sticky and sweet, tangy and rich with umami, with just a touch of heat. While my mom's OG sweet and sour sauce (page 57) is simpler and the perfect accompaniment to fan favorites like egg rolls, I like to think of this tamarind sauce as a punchier and tangier version, thanks to the acidity of the tamarind. Both find that balance of sweet and salty, but if you want a sauce that's a little bit funkier thanks to the inclusion of fish sauce, this will be your go-to.

- **1½ cups (395 g) tamarind concentrate**
- **2 (2-ounce / 55 g) disks palm sugar**
- **2 tablespoons fish sauce**
- **¾ cup (150 g) granulated sugar**
- **½ teaspoon kosher salt**
- **2 tablespoons cornstarch**

In a medium saucepan, combine the tamarind, palm sugar, fish sauce, granulated sugar, salt, and 5 tablespoons (75 ml) water and cook over medium-low heat, stirring to break up any palm sugar clumps, until both sugars are completely dissolved, about 5 minutes.

Meanwhile, make a cornstarch slurry: In a small bowl, combine the cornstarch and 2 tablespoons water and whisk until the cornstarch is fully dissolved.

Whisk the slurry into the simmering liquid and cook until the sauce thickens like a syrup or honey, about 2 minutes. Remove from the heat and let cool.

Store in an airtight container (like a lidded glass jar) in the refrigerator for up to 1 month.

DUMPLING SAUCE
OG SWEET + SOUR SAUCE
TAMARIND SAUCE
MOM'S HOT SAUCE

Sauce Gai

Sweet Chile Sauce

Makes 2 cups (480 ml)

You can buy this sauce bottled (Mae Ploy is probably the most popular and well-known version), but why not try making it from scratch? It's easy, plus you can adjust the sweetness and the spice completely—just use this recipe as a guideline. And when you're finished, make sure you've got your egg rolls, crab rangoons, and fried chicken lined up for a dip.

- 2 tablespoons cornstarch
- 2 tablespoons ketchup
- 1 tablespoon finely chopped garlic
- 1 tablespoon chopped, peeled fresh ginger (about a 1-inch / 2.5 cm knob)
- 1 teaspoon Prik Pohn (Toasted Ground Chile, page 54) or crushed dried Thai chile (from about 1 chile)
- ¼ teaspoon kosher salt
- 1 cup (200 g) sugar
- 1 cup (240 ml) distilled white vinegar

First, make a cornstarch slurry: In a small bowl, combine the cornstarch and 3 tablespoons water and whisk until the cornstarch is fully dissolved.

In a medium saucepan, combine the ketchup, garlic, ginger, prik pohn, salt, sugar, vinegar, and ¼ cup (60 ml) water and bring to a simmer over medium-low heat. Reduce the sauce by one-third, about 6 minutes, to cook out the tartness of the vinegar. Whisk in the cornstarch slurry and cook until thickened, about 2 minutes. Let cool before serving.

Store in an airtight container (like a lidded glass jar) in the refrigerator for up to 1 week.

Sriracha

Makes 1¼ cups (300 ml)

Never stress during a sriracha shortage again. A lot of folks don't know this, but this chile sauce actually hails from a city in Thailand called, well, Si Racha. The Thai version is different from the red rooster version you may have seen stateside, which is more acidic and plainly hot. Thai sriracha strikes a balance between spice and sweetness and has a much more rounded flavor with a punchiness from garlic. You can adapt this recipe to be as spicy as you want; the version I've produced is my perfect, happy medium.

- 4 red jalapeño chiles (4 ounces / 115 g) (or Fresno chiles for a milder sauce)
- 2¾ cups (60 g) dried Thai chiles
- 2½ cups (60 g) dried arbol chiles
- 6 cloves garlic, peeled
- 2 cups (480 ml) white distilled vinegar
- 1 cup (220 g) packed light brown sugar
- 1 teaspoon kosher salt

In the base of a blender, combine the jalapeños, Thai chiles, arbol chiles, garlic, vinegar, brown sugar, salt, and ½ cup (120 ml) water and blend until mostly smooth. Transfer the sauce to a lidded glass jar and lightly cover with plastic wrap.

Place the jar on a windowsill in direct sunlight for 3 to 4 days, allowing the mixture to lightly bubble and ferment.

Strain the sauce through a fine-mesh sieve, stirring and pushing on the solids to release every last drop (about 2¼ cups / 540 ml), into a small saucepan. Place over low heat, bring to a simmer, and simmer, stirring occasionally, until reduced by one-third and thickened enough to what's known as a *nappe consistency*, or so it can coat the back of a spoon, about 30 minutes. Remove from the heat and let cool.

Store in an airtight container (like a li dded glass jar) in the refrigerator for up to 3 weeks.

SRIRACHA
SAUCE GAI

Garnishes & Flourishes

Pickled Garlic and Vinegar

Makes 1 cup (90 g) pickled garlic and 3 cups (720 ml) garlic vinegar

This is for my pickle lovers and my garlic lovers—why not combine the two and have pickled garlic? This garnish has plenty of thinly sliced garlic, vinegar, a little bit of sugar, and some salt to round it out. It's easy to prepare and adds so much dimension drizzled over a bowl of noodle soup or stir-fried glass noodles. Its aromatic flavor not only balances rich stews but also brightens lighter dishes. You'll want to put this on everything.

- 2 tablespoons sugar
- 1 tablespoon kosher salt
- 1 cup (120 g) thinly sliced garlic (about 45 cloves)
- 2 cups (480 ml) distilled white vinegar

In a small saucepan, combine 1 cup (240 ml) water, the sugar, and salt. Place over medium heat and stir until the sugar and salt are completely dissolved. Remove from the heat.

Place the sliced garlic into a large heatproof container or lidded glass jar and pour the sugar mixture over the garlic. Add the vinegar and stir to combine. Let the liquid cool completely in the refrigerator, about 24 hours, before using.

Store at room temperature for up to 2 weeks or refrigerate for up to 1 month.

Khao Kuah
Toasted Rice Powder

Makes ½ cup (100 g)

Toasted rice powder, or khao kuah, is so easy to prepare and adds a hit of nuttiness to everything it touches. This is what gives laab and other herbaceous Thai salads a greater depth of flavor. Trust me, it's noticeable when it's not there. Yes, you can purchase it at an Asian grocery store, but it's so easy to make yourself that you should never skip it. An added benefit of making rice powder at home is that toasting releases the fragrant aroma of browned rice, which will make your house smell delicious.

- ½ cup (100 g) raw jasmine long-grain or sticky rice

In a dry skillet, toast the rice over low heat, tossing, until golden brown, about 10 minutes. Set aside to cool.

In a mortar with pestle or spice grinder, grind the toasted rice until the texture is similar to coarse sand, 3 to 5 minutes in a mortar (and roughly 30 seconds in a spice grinder).

Store in an airtight container (like a lidded glass jar) for up to 6 months.

GARLIC OIL
PICKLED GARLIC
FRIED SHALLOT
RICE POWDER

Fried Shallots

Makes 1 cup (60 g)

The perfect garnish in Thai cooking is a crown of fried shallots. You can sprinkle them over noodle soups, jhok, fried chicken—sometimes even on desserts. They're simple to make and add a touch of sweetness and crunch to every dish they touch. Keep in mind that it's important to slice the shallots evenly for consistent cooking. You can use a mandoline if you'd like (please be careful!), but I prefer wielding my knife. And if you don't want to fry shallots yourself, you can find jarred fried shallots at Asian grocery stores.

- 2 cups (480 ml) neutral oil, such as sunflower
- 1 cup (100 g) thinly sliced shallots (about 4 shallots)
- ½ teaspoon kosher salt

Preheat the oven to 300°F (150°C). In a medium saucepan, heat the oil over high heat until a thermometer reads 350°F (175°C).

In a medium bowl, toss the shallots with the salt. Place the shallots in a single layer between two paper towels and let stand for 5 minutes. Lightly press on the paper towels to remove any liquid from the shallots.

Using a fine-mesh sieve or spider, gently place a few slices of shallot into the hot oil, and once they start to bubble, reduce the heat until the oil temperature goes down to 300°F (150°C). Working in small batches, add the shallots to the oil, allowing them to dance around and lightly brown and being careful not to overcrowd the pan to maintain the oil temperature. Fry, stirring occasionally, until the shallots begin to turn pale golden, about 3 minutes (they will get darker as they sit). Transfer the shallots to a paper towel–lined baking sheet or plate to remove excess oil. Repeat with the remaining shallots (see Note).

Gently pat the shallots with a paper towel to remove any remaining oil. Transfer the fried shallots to a baking sheet and bake until dry and crispier, 3 to 5 minutes.

Use immediately, or store the fried shallots in an airtight container for up to 7 days.

Note: You can reserve the oil used for cooking the shallots. This flavorful oil comes in handy for sautéing meats or vegetables, or when making the dishes in the wok cooking chapter (see page 122), for example.

Fried Garlic and Garlic Oil

Makes ½ cup (70 g) fried garlic and 2 cups (480 ml) garlic oil

Fried garlic is an essential topping in Thai cuisine, but trust me when I say you'll want to put this on everything. And while you can purchase fried garlic, the best part of making this is that it's a two-for-one recipe. Yes, you'll get golden brown flecks of garlic that you can sprinkle on jhok, noodles, and fried chicken, but you'll also get the residual oil the garlic was cooked in, which becomes imbued with a punchy garlic aroma. Use the oil for fried rice or to cook any protein. To speed up the process, you can pulse eighteen cloves garlic in a food processor until evenly chopped.

½ cup (70 g) chopped garlic
2 cups (480 ml) neutral oil, such as sunflower
¼ teaspoon kosher salt

In a medium saucepan, combine the garlic and oil. Place over medium heat and cook, stirring with a wooden spoon, until the garlic starts to bubble, about 5 minutes. Increase the heat to high and cook, stirring occasionally, until the garlic starts to dance around and turns a pale golden color, about another 2 minutes. Immediately remove the pan from the heat. The garlic will continue to brown and crisp while the oil is cooling. Using a fine-mesh strainer, remove the garlic before it looks completely crispy and golden brown to avoid burning. (Be aware that the garlic can burn and turn bitter quickly, so it is crucial to remove the garlic before this happens.)

Transfer the garlic to a paper towel–lined plate to absorb any excess oil. Sprinkle the crispy garlic with the salt. Cool completely.

Use immediately, or store the fried garlic in an airtight container for up to 7 days. Store the garlic-infused oil in an airtight container (such as a lidded jar) for up to 2 weeks. (In addition to this crispy fried garlic, I also like to reserve the oil with bits of the fried garlic in the same container for a bonus garnish that's great when added to soups and noodles).

PRODUCT
ROLLIE
FOCO

I've Got Ninety-Nine Recipes, and Pad Thai Ain't One

If you flip through the pages of this book hoping for a pad Thai recipe, I've got some bad news for you: You won't find it here. It's true—I have ninety-nine recipes (actually, it ended up being one hundred), but not one of them is what is considered Thailand's national dish. It's not that I abhor pad Thai or that I don't know how to make it (trust me, it is by far the best-selling item on my thirty-dish menu at International Market). It's just that I'm bored of it. Pad Thai is on every menu of practically every Thai restaurant in America, and recipes for the dish are a dime a dozen. When it came to writing this cookbook, I didn't want to give my readers something that felt redundant. I also didn't want to write a recipe for a dish I'm not excited about.

I am so, so grateful that pad Thai keeps the lights on at IM and that it is often a gateway dish for many to the beautiful world of Thai cuisine. I owe a lot to pad Thai, and I know Thai food enthusiasts everywhere do, too. I get it—pad Thai is a comfort. But at the same time, eventually we must let go of our security blankets.

Pad Thai started appearing on menus in the US back in the eighties and nineties, when Thai immigrants first came stateside and began popularizing the dish. It is said that pad Thai was initially developed by the Thai government in the wake of World War II to not only extend the life of rice during shortages, but also to serve as a unifying dish representative of all of Thailand. Pad Thai was inspired by the influx of Chinese migrants and the fried noodle dish kway teow that they brought with them, which eventually evolved to suit Thai taste buds with the addition of tamarind sauce, pickled radish, and chiles. There are Thai people out there who love pad Thai, but neither I nor my coauthor fit into this category. The fact that its introduction to the world was through a nationalist policy has always felt slightly off-putting to me. I often refer to pad Thai as the pumpkin spice latte of our menu: comforting, sweet, and nostalgic, sure, but undeniably basic.

The pad Thai you are getting stateside is often nothing like the kind you'll find in Thailand. Pad Thai should not be orange and gloopy; instead, it should have visible char marks and a complex aroma from tamarind, palm sugar, and fish sauce, and include a confetti of textural ingredients like preserved radish, dried shrimp, garlic chives, and bean sprouts. I'm all for fusion takes on this classic dish, like incorporating crispy pork belly or lobster as the predominant protein or making an extra-spicy version, but I just can't stomach an overly saucy dish that tastes like syrup.

I know my mom had to include pad Thai in International Market's menu to appease her clientele, and I've kept it on the menu because it's so beloved, but she'd be so proud to see how far the restaurant, and I, have come. She'd be thrilled to know I'm including a stink bean recipe in these pages (page 144), or that I'm teaching you all how to make a funky bamboo shoot stew (page 78). My progress is her progress, and I'm excited to show you a different side of Thai food—*my* side of Thai food.

CHAPTER 4 ◆ DIPS & SUCH

You might not necessarily associate Thai food with dips. Maybe a Mexican cookbook would seem more appropriate to have an entire chapter devoted to this category—guacamole, salsa, bean dip, and the like. But I'm here to tell you that Thai dips should not be missed. They are on almost every table of a home-cooked Thai meal or prepared for afternoon snacking. There are spicy dips, of course, but also funky fishy dips, sour dips, and dips intended for fruits. You can dive into these dips with just about anything, but the most classic pairings are sliced cucumber, raw green beans, cabbage, fried pork rinds, and freshly steamed sticky rice. Some dips are more like a centerpiece, like my chunky eggplant dip (page 82) and stewed bamboo shoots (page 78). Others function as an accompaniment to larger spreads of food but are still mandatory (like my dried chile sauce on page 72). In Thailand, it's not unheard of to have a breakfast of sticky rice, a dip, and vegetables. There's a dip specifically for seafood, and I've even gotten a little fancy and prepared my signature peanut sauce as a special fondue (page 70). I'm excited to introduce you to Thailand's magical world of dips.

Peanut Sauce Fondue

Makes 3 cups (420 ml)

The hype for my peanut sauce is real. At the restaurant, diners always want a side of peanut sauce, even for dishes that I wouldn't typically pair with it. Every iteration of "Thai" salad out there from chain restaurants has a peanut sauce because people can't get enough of the creamy dressing. I get it—the combination of sweet, salty, and a little bit of heat is entirely craveable, especially when put next to coconut milk–kissed satay. But peanut sauce can be so much more than a foil to skewers. Thais love it with a side of toast, and it would also be great tossed with hot noodles and a splash of vinegar. What I personally love to do is set it up like fondue, with a spread of fresh veggies, toast, and skewers. It makes for a fun and interactive meal, all centered on this nutty sauce. It even tastes great when paired with potato chips and would make a fabulous addition to any game-day spread. To sexy it up, you can swirl in a drizzle of coconut, add crushed peanuts on top, and sprinkle a chiffonade of makrut lime leaves for some color. And if you want to eat it by the spoonful, I won't judge.

2 tablespoons neutral oil, such as sunflower

¼ cup (35 g) finely chopped white onion

4 fresh makrut lime leaves, ribs removed and torn into small pieces

4 cloves garlic, finely chopped

1 tablespoon Prik Pohn (Toasted Ground Chile, page 54) or crushed dried Thai chile (about 6 chiles)

3 tablespoons red curry paste

2 tablespoons tamarind concentrate, plus more for seasoning

1½ cups (365 g) extra-crunchy peanut butter

2 tablespoons fish sauce

1 tablespoon sugar

¼ cup (60 ml) sweet soy sauce

For serving:

Coconut milk

Chile crisp

Thinly sliced scallions

Assorted vegetables

In a medium saucepan, heat the oil over medium heat until it shimmers. Add the onion and cook until softened, about 2 minutes. Add the makrut lime leaves, garlic, and prik pohn and cook down a bit, whisking so as not to burn the garlic, about 30 seconds. Add the red curry paste and tamarind concentrate and cook just to heat the paste, about 1 minute. Add the peanut butter and ¾ cup (180 ml) water to thin out the sauce and stir until it reaches a thick gravy consistency. Reduce the heat to low and stir in the fish sauce, sugar, and sweet soy sauce. Remove from the heat and season with a bit more tamarind, if needed.

If the sauce is too thick, add more water, 1 tablespoon at a time, to thin it out. If the sauce breaks and the oil separates, remove it from the heat and, once cooled, whip it with a whisk until it reaches your desired creamy texture. Adding a splash of cold water will help, too.

TO SERVE:

Swirl in coconut milk and garnish with chile crisp and scallions. Serve warm with assorted vegetables for dipping.

Store in an airtight container (like a lidded glass jar) in the refrigerator for up to 1 week. Reheat before serving, whisking, to incorporate any oil that may have separated, if necessary.

Nam Jim Jaeow
Dried Chile Sauce

Makes 1 cup (240 ml)

Every Thai family has their own recipe for nam jim jaeow, and everyone thinks theirs is the best. This chile sauce hails from the Isaan region of Thailand and pairs well with crying tiger (Thai-style grilled steak), barbecue chicken, fatty strips of pork cheek, and nuah daad diew, our beef jerky (page 110). Like most Thai food, nam jim jaeow is about striking a perfect balance: There is spicy heat, nutty toasted rice powder, bright acidity from tamarind, pungency from fish sauce, and a generous kick of garlic. I balance my version out with sugar and add herbaceousness with cilantro and shallots. It's so good that you don't even need a protein to enjoy it—just get your hands on some sticky rice and take a dip.

- ¼ cup (50 g) sugar
- ¼ cup (60 ml) fish sauce
- ¼ cup (70 g) tamarind concentrate
- ¼ cup (60 ml) Thai seasoning sauce
- 2 tablespoons minced garlic
- 2 tablespoons minced, peeled fresh ginger
- ½ tablespoon Prik Pohn (Toasted Ground Chile, page 54) or crushed dried Thai chile (about 3 chiles)
- Khao Kuah (Toasted Rice Powder, page 62), for serving (optional)

In a medium bowl, combine the sugar, fish sauce, tamarind, Thai seasoning sauce, garlic, ginger, and prik pohn and whisk until the sugar is fully dissolved, about 3 minutes. Sprinkle with khao kuah before serving, if desired.

Store in an airtight container (like a lidded glass jar) in the refrigerator for up to 1 week.

CLOCKWISE FROM TOP:
Nam Prik Grapi (page 74),
Nam Jim Talay (page 75),
Nam Jim Jaeow (opposite)

Nam Prik Grapi
Shrimp Paste Chile Dip

Makes ¾ cup (205 g)

I won't mince words: If you're not used to the funkiness of fermented fishy products, this dip can definitely clear a room. It's prepared with a grayish aged shrimp paste and is unapologetically stinky in the best way. That's what makes it so special! To some, the scent may be challenging, but it sets off my salivary glands like nothing else. To cut through the fishiness, Thai eggplant, chiles, and garlic are tossed in. The turkey berry eggplants, which are small and shaped like grapes, add a welcome pop of bitterness. Serve this with steamed or fresh veggies, grilled fish, Thai-style omelets, rice, and even pork rinds!

12 fresh red Thai chiles

4 cloves garlic, peeled

½ teaspoon neutral oil, such as sunflower

2 tablespoons shrimp paste

2 (2-ounce / 55 g) disks palm sugar

1 Thai eggplant, thinly sliced (about 2 ounces / 55 g), or ideally 12 fresh turkey berry eggplants from an Asian market, if available (sometimes called pea eggplants)

¼ cup (60 ml) fresh lime juice

Adjust a rack 5 to 6 inches (12 to 15 cm) from your oven's heat source and preheat the broiler.

In a small bowl, lightly toss the Thai chiles and garlic with the oil. Spread out the chiles and garlic on a baking pan and broil until toasted and slightly charred, 3 to 5 minutes.

Place the shrimp paste on a large piece of foil and close the edges around the paste to form a packet. Broil until darker and pungent, 3 to 5 minutes.

Using a mortar with a pestle, pound the broiled chiles and garlic with the roasted shrimp paste and palm sugar until a coarse paste forms, about 3 minutes. Add the eggplant and lightly pound everything together, 1 to 2 minutes (the eggplant will still be chunky). Stir in the lime juice and transfer to a serving bowl.

Serve immediately or store in an airtight container (like a lidded glass jar) in the refrigerator for up to 5 days.

Nam Jim Talay
Thai Seafood Sauce

Makes 1 cup (240 ml)

If it were up to us Thais, every Las Vegas buffet or seafood boil restaurant would have nam jim talay available. This is the seafood sauce you'll find at both beachside Thai restaurants in the most touristy places in Thailand and local holes-in-the-wall that specialize in grilled giant river prawns. It's the go-to sauce to add to seafood. And when I say seafood, I mean every type of seafood—prawns, shrimp, cockles, squid, fish, lobster, oysters—however it is prepared, whether it is grilled, steamed, fried, or stir-fried. Lime juice, Thai chiles, garlic, and fish sauce lend this dip so much zippy flavor, I feel like I can't enjoy seafood without it.

- ½ cup (120 ml) fresh lime juice
- ¼ cup (60 ml) fish sauce
- ¼ cup (50 g) sugar
- 1 tablespoon minced garlic
- 1 tablespoon chopped fresh Thai chile, or to taste
- ¼ cup (16 g) roughly chopped fresh cilantro leaves
- 2 tablespoons roughly chopped fresh dill
- 2 scallions, green and white parts, thinly sliced

In a medium bowl, combine the lime juice, fish sauce, sugar, garlic, and Thai chile and whisk until the sugar is completely dissolved, about 3 minutes. When ready to serve, add the cilantro, dill, and scallions and stir to combine.

Serve immediately or store in an airtight container (like a lidded glass jar) in the refrigerator for up to 1 week.

Nam Prik Klang Dong
Caramelized Dried Shrimp and Anchovy Crumble

Makes 4 cups (450 g)

Nam prik klang dong is one of many versions of nam prik in Thailand (and also in this book, as you may have noticed). The term *nam prik* is a catchall phrase for chile paste, but the consistency varies across different styles. Some are chunkier, like a pico de gallo, while others are sticky and jammy. This particular version translates to "chile dip in the middle of the jungle," and is special because it's not pasty or wet but rather dry and crispy, almost like Chex or trail mix or even a Thai version of Japanese togarashi (a spice blend of ground dried chiles, citrus, sesame seeds, and other seasonings). I love to enjoy it simply in the same way togarashi is typically used—to season a piping hot bowl of steamed rice. You can also sprinkle this over salads and fried eggs. When my family would travel on long trips back in the day, nothing beat a ball of sticky rice to dip into this savory flavor explosion.

- 2 tablespoons neutral oil, such as sunflower
- 2 cups (260 g) chopped red onions
- ½ cup (40 g) chopped fresh cilantro stems
- 3½ ounces (100 g) dried shrimp (1¼ cups)
- 4 ounces (115 g) dried anchovies (2 cups)
- ½ ounce (14 g) dried Thai chiles (about ½ cup)
- 2 cups (120 g) Fried Shallots (page 64), or store-bought fried shallots
- 3 whole fresh makrut lime leaves (ribs removed)
- ¼ cup (60 ml) fish sauce
- ½ cup (100 g) sugar
- 1 tablespoon thinly sliced fresh makrut lime leaves (ribs removed)

Preheat the oven to 200°F (90°C).

In a large skillet, heat the oil over medium heat. Add the onions and cook, stirring occasionally, until browned and almost caramelized, about 25 minutes. Add the cilantro stems, shrimp, anchovies, Thai chiles, fried shallots, and whole lime leaves. Cook, stirring, for 2 minutes. Stir in the fish sauce and sugar and mix until evenly combined. Remove from the heat and add thinly sliced lime leaves.

Transfer to a large baking pan and spread into a thin and even layer. Bake until the mixture is dry and crispy, 1 to 1½ hours. Remove from the oven and let cool completely. Wearing gloves, crumble the chiles and toss to evenly combine.

Serve immediately or store in an airtight container (like a lidded glass jar) at room temperature for up to 2 weeks.

Om Nawmai
Stewed Bamboo Shoot Dip

Makes about 4 cups (960 ml)

This is a favorite among the aunties who have been running International Market since before I was born. Eating this dip is also one of my fondest memories from my childhood. And even today, whenever I am searching for a snack, my aunties will most likely have some version of this dish packed in their daily survival kit, a lunchbox complete with sticky rice. It's easy to understand why—it's funky and spicy, and the tangy bamboo shoots give it a pickle-like flavor. Traditionally, this dish is made with an extract from the yanang leaf as well with an occasional hint of cha-om, but my quick-fix version is inspired by the dish's Laotian heritage so it includes plenty of mushrooms and Thai chiles. And the texture! The bamboo shoots maintain their bite despite being stewed. If you've ever found yourself with a can of bamboo shoots with no idea what to do with them, make this. It might not be as good as my aunties' version, but it gets me through until our next meal together.

14-ounces / 400 g bamboo shoot tips (about 10 tips), prepared (see Note, page 18)

½ cup (60 g) thinly sliced red onion (from about ½ red onion)

8 fresh green Thai chiles, stems removed

2 stalks lemongrass (about 4 ounces / 100 g), ends trimmed, tough outer layers removed, and thinly sliced

4 ounces (115 g) heirloom mushrooms, such as oyster and beech mushrooms, torn

2 tablespoons Khao Kuah (Toasted Rice Powder, page 62)

2 tablespoons fish sauce

1 teaspoon sugar

½ teaspoon Magic Powder (aka Asian chicken bouillon)

1 large bunch fresh dill, stalks torn into thirds

1 cup (30 g) packed fresh Thai basil leaves, torn

For serving:

Fresh cilantro leaves

Sticky Rice (page 38)

Using two forks, shred the prepared bamboo shoots into smaller strips, similar to how you would pull pork or chicken.

In a mortar with a pestle, pound the onion, Thai chiles, and half of the lemongrass together until lightly crushed, about 1 minute.

Pour 2 cups (480 ml) water into a medium saucepan and bring to a boil over high heat. Add the pounded Thai chile-onion mixture, the bamboo shoots, mushrooms, the remaining lemongrass, khao kuah, fish sauce, sugar, and magic powder. Reduce the heat and simmer, stirring occasionally, until the mushrooms begin to wilt and soften, about 3 minutes. Add the dill and cook for 2 minutes. Stir in the Thai basil and remove from the heat.

TO SERVE:

Serve warm or at room temperature, topped with cilantro and with a side of sticky rice. Store in an airtight container (like a lidded glass jar) in the refrigerator for up to 5 days.

Small
Cottage
4% MILKFAT

Nam Prik Ong
Tomato and Ground Pork Dip

Serves 4

This pounded chile dip featuring ground pork or chicken, shrimp paste, and lots of tomatoes, garlic, and shallots packs so much flavor in a singular dip. Although it's bright red, it's not as spicy as some of the other dips in Thailand's culinary canon. Eat this with crunchy raw vegetables, like sliced cucumber, green beans, quartered Thai eggplant, cabbage wedges, or endive; pork rinds; or even a steaming bowl of rice—I like to add a soft-boiled egg to make it a complete meal.

- 3 dried Thai chiles
- 5 cloves garlic, peeled
- Kosher salt
- 1½ teaspoons shrimp paste
- ¼ bunch fresh cilantro, leaves and stems, chopped
- 1 cup (200 g) cherry tomatoes, halved
- 1 tablespoon neutral oil, such as sunflower
- ¼ cup (30 g) chopped red onion or shallots
- 8 ounces (225 g) ground pork (or chicken)
- 1 scallion, green and white parts, sliced, plus additional for serving

Place the dried Thai chiles in a small bowl and pour warm water over them to rehydrate. Let them stand for 10 minutes.

In a mortar with a pestle, grind the garlic cloves, rehydrated Thai chiles, and a teaspoon of salt until broken down and combined. Add the shrimp paste and a small handful of the cilantro and tomato until a coarse paste is formed.

In a large skillet, heat the oil over low heat. Add the onion and cook until it begins to soften and turn pale, about 3 minutes. Add the garlic-chile paste and stir until fragrant and well combined, about 1 minute. Add the rest of the tomatoes to the pan and lightly stir until the tomatoes begin to break down.

Add the pork and cook, lightly stirring until no longer pink and cooked through, about 6 minutes. Add the scallions, remaining cilantro, and up to ½ cup (120 ml) water, 1 tablespoon at a time, until the mixture reaches a thick consistency, similar to a Bolognese or the filling for a Sloppy Joe sandwich.

Serve warm in a bowl with a sprinkle of scallions, or let cool then store in an airtight container (like a lidded glass jar) in the refrigerator for up to 3 days.

Jaeow Makuah
Roasted Eggplant Dip

Makes 2 cups (480 g)

This recipe is a shout out to the ladies who raised me. I grew up eating this roasted eggplant dip in the kitchen of my mom's restaurant with her cooks. I like to think of it as Thailand's answer to baba ghanoush—but with a more roasted flavor and a spicy kick. The traditional method is to pound it in a mortar and pestle, but you can also blitz it in a food processor. This dip can easily be made vegan by omitting the shrimp paste and is stellar paired with sticky rice, pork rinds, jammy eggs, and fresh vegetables, such as cucumber, okra, carrots, green beans, and/or cabbage.

- 2 Japanese eggplants or 1 small Italian eggplant, split lengthwise (about 1 pound / 455 g)
- 2 Anaheim chiles, stems removed
- 2 jalapeño chiles, stems removed
- 4 cloves garlic, peeled
- 3 shallots (6 ounces / 170 g) or ½ red onion, quartered and peeled
- 1 teaspoon neutral oil, such as sunflower
- 1½ teaspoons shrimp paste
- ¼ bunch fresh cilantro stems, chopped
- 1 tablespoon Prik Pohn (Toasted Ground Chile, page 54) or crushed dried Thai chile (about 8 chiles)
- 1 tablespoon fresh lime juice
- 1½ teaspoons sugar
- 1½ teaspoons Magic Powder (aka Asian chicken bouillon)

Adjust a rack 5 to 6 inches (12 to 15 cm) from your oven's heat source and preheat the broiler to high.

On a baking pan, gently toss the eggplant, Anaheim chiles, jalapeño chiles, garlic, and shallots with the oil. Place the eggplant flesh-side down on the pan and broil until the eggplant skin is charred and the chiles are roasted, about 8 minutes. (Alternatively, if you have a gas stove, you could roast the eggplant over your stove's open flame to char the skin). Let cool then remove and discard the charred skin from the eggplant. Reserve the flesh and set aside.

Place the shrimp paste on a large piece of foil and close the edges around the paste to form a packet. Broil in the oven until darker and pungent, 3 to 5 minutes.

In a mortar with a pestle, pound the roasted chiles, shallots, and garlic with the cilantro stems into a coarse paste, about 5 minutes. Add the broiled shrimp paste, prik pohn, and the reserved eggplant flesh and pound together until fully incorporated, about 8 minutes. Stir in the lime juice, sugar, and magic powder until evenly combined.

Transfer the mixture to a bowl and serve, or store in an airtight container (like a lidded glass jar) in the refrigerator for up to 5 days.

Nam Pla Wahn

Dried Shrimp and Chile Fish Sauce Caramel

Makes about 1 cup (395 g)

People think mango season in Thailand is all about mango sticky rice, but they're wrong. Mango season is for green mangoes paired with nam pla wan, this sticky, salty, caramel-like dip that features pungent dried shrimp and plenty of shallots. When I get a whiff of this stuff, my mouth immediately waters. It's the perfect foil to tart and crisp green mango, as well as guava and green apples. You'll never look at fruit the same after trying this dip.

- **3½ ounces (100 g) dried shrimp (about 1¼ cups)**
- **¼ bunch fresh cilantro stems, chopped**
- **12 whole dried Thai chiles**
- **8 fresh red Thai chiles, stems removed**
- **1 teaspoon shrimp paste**
- **3 shallots (6 ounces / 170 g), thinly sliced**
- **2 (2-ounce / 55 g) disks palm sugar**
- **¼ cup (50 g) granulated sugar**
- **¼ cup (60 ml) fish sauce**
- **24 fresh cilantro leaves**

In a mortar with a pestle, lightly pound together the dried shrimp, cilantro stems, dried Thai chiles, Thai chiles, and shrimp paste until the chiles are broken down, about 8 minutes. Set aside.

In a medium saucepan, combine the shallots, palm sugar, granulated sugar, fish sauce, and ¼ cup (60 ml) water and bring to a simmer over medium heat. Simmer, stirring, until the sugars are dissolved, 4 to 5 minutes.

Add the reserved shrimp-chile mixture to the pan and simmer until the flavors marry and the liquid begins to thicken, about 1 minute.

Remove from the heat and, using a rubber spatula, fold in the cilantro leaves. Transfer to a bowl and serve immediately, or store in an airtight container (like a lidded glass jar) in the refrigerator for up to 5 days.

CHAPTER 5 ◆ SNACKS & SMALLS

Thai people are unbelievably snacky. Don't believe me? Take a look at any night market in Thailand—the overwhelming majority of vendors are selling little bites, everything from bubbly seafood pancakes to shiny, spherical tapioca dumplings, foods that are meant to tide you over between meals or can be combined to make a snack feast. If that's not convincing enough, go to a Thai 7-Eleven, an underappreciated haven for Thai snacking, where you can find a stunning array of packaged goodies like seaweed snacks and potato chips in a rainbow of colors and flavors and prepared foods like dumplings and meat skewers. In a culture enamored with food, snacking is one of our national pastimes.

And I'm not immune; I love a good snack. Snacks are what kept me going through late nights feeding my daughter and what I have before dinner service to keep me satiated before closing. Snacks remind me of my mom and her award-winning egg rolls (page 88) or my grandma's perfect hand-shaped dumplings (page 92). For your next snack attack, I will share some of my favorites.

Mom's Egg Rolls

Makes about 10 egg rolls

Egg rolls, to my mom, were currency. For the longest time, they rang in at $1 a pop, and anytime I'd ask for anything, my mom would remind me of how many egg rolls she'd have to sell to afford my toys, school supplies, or new shoes. It's funny that she thought about them as money because, in all honesty, this egg roll recipe is worth its weight in gold. I was raised on the sales of these egg rolls, and I hope you appreciate them as much as I do.

For the filling:

- 4 ounces (115 g) dry bean thread glass noodles
- ¼ cup (10 g) dried mushrooms, such as wood ear or shiitake
- 2 tablespoons neutral oil, such as sunflower, plus additional for frying (about 8 cups / 2 liters)
- 2 cups (165 g) shredded green cabbage
- ½ cup (55 g) chopped white onion
- 1 (8-ounce / 225 g) can bamboo shoot strips, prepared per instructions on page 18
- 2 tablespoons black soy sauce
- 1 tablespoon sugar
- ½ teaspoon kosher salt
- ¼ teaspoon Magic Powder (aka Asian chicken bouillon)

For the egg rolls:

- 10 to 12 sheets egg roll wrappers, thawed according to package instructions, if frozen

For serving:

- International Market OG Sweet and Sour Sauce (page 57)

MAKE THE FILLING:

Put the noodles in a large bowl, add 4 cups (960 ml) hot water, and soak until softened, about 20 minutes. Drain the noodles, pat them dry, and, using kitchen scissors, cut into roughly 2-inch (5 cm) pieces. In a small bowl, soak the dried mushrooms in warm water until softened, about 10 minutes. Drain, pat dry, and cut into thin slices.

In a large skillet, heat the oil over medium heat. Add the cabbage, onion, bamboo shoots, mushrooms, bean thread noodles, black soy sauce, sugar, salt, and magic powder and stir to combine. Cook, stirring occasionally, until the cabbage is wilted, about 10 minutes. Remove from the heat and let the mixture cool, about 20 minutes.

ROLL THE EGG ROLLS:

Fill a small bowl with cool water. Keeping the wrappers covered with a damp kitchen or paper towel, place a wrapper on a clean work surface, in a diamond shape with one point facing the bottom edge of the surface. Place about ¼ cup (60 g) of the mixture on the bottom half of the wrapper, closest to you. Pull the bottom point up, over, and tuck under the filling, and tightly roll the wrapper away from you. When you reach the middle, fold the side points into the center, and continue tightly rolling away from you, stopping a couple inches from the top. Using your finger or a brush, rub a little water along the edges of the wrapper and roll until sealed. Repeat with the remaining filling and wrappers, covering the rolls with a damp towel as you go.

Meanwhile, pour enough oil to come 1½ inches (4 cm) up the sides of a deep saucepan and heat over medium heat until a deep-fry thermometer reads 375°F (190°C).

COOK THE EGG ROLLS:

Using a spider or slotted spoon, gently place a few egg rolls in the hot oil, working in batches to prevent overcrowding, and cook until the wrappers turn light golden brown, 1 to 2 minutes. Transfer them to a wire rack. Repeat with the remaining egg rolls.

TO SERVE:

Serve the rolls immediately with a side of sweet and sour sauce.

CLOCKWISE FROM TOP: Mom's Egg Rolls (opposite), International Market OG Sweet and Sour Sauce (page 57), Khanom Pang Tod (page 90), Cucumber Achaar (page 196), Mom's Chicken Wontons (page 91)

Khanom Pang Tod
Shrimp Toast

Makes 4 pieces

It's impossible to deny the appeal of fried bread, especially when the bread has a generous smear of shrimp on it. My mom introduced this dish to International Market back in the eighties, mixing pork with imitation crab before battering the entire thing in egg and deep-frying it. The dish is inspired by the Chinese takeout classic and also references the popular Thai snack khanom pang na moo, a similar fried bread appetizer that uses ground pork instead of imitation crab. I've since made my own adaptations to my mom's earlier version by swapping the imitation crab for shrimp and including water chestnuts for added crunch.

- 8 ounces (225 g) large shrimp, shelled and deveined
- ½ cup (58 g) chopped celery
- ½ cup (55 g) chopped white onion
- ½ cup (56 g) water chestnuts, roughly chopped
- 1 tablespoon oyster sauce
- ½ teaspoon garlic powder
- 1 teaspoon sugar
- ½ teaspoon ground white pepper
- 1 teaspoon Magic Powder (aka Asian chicken bouillon)
- 2 tablespoons rice flour
- 4 bread slices, such as baguette or Texas toast
- 1 to 2 tablespoons neutral oil, such as sunflower

For serving:

- Sesame seeds
- International Market OG Sweet and Sour Sauce (page 57)
- Cucumber Achaar (page 196)

Pulse the shrimp in a food processor until it has a texture resembling ground beef. Add the celery, onion, water chestnuts, oyster sauce, garlic powder, sugar, white pepper, magic powder, and rice flour and pulse until evenly combined, being cautious not to overprocess the mixture to smooth (texture and chunks are a good thing).

Evenly spread ½ cup (60 g) of the shrimp mixture on one side of a slice of bread, about ¼ inch (6 mm) thick. Repeat with the remaining slices and refrigerate for 15 minutes to set.

Meanwhile, preheat the oven to 350°F (175°C).

Add enough oil to a large skillet to coat the bottom and heat over medium heat. Gently place the toast mixture-side down into the oil (work in batches if necessary) and cook until lightly golden underneath, about 1 minute. Using a flat spatula, carefully flip the toast and cook until golden brown and crispy on the other side, about another 30 seconds.

Remove the toast slices from the skillet and transfer to a baking pan, shrimp sides up. Bake until cooked through and crisp on top, 1 to 2 minutes.

TO SERVE:

Transfer to a platter and serve warm topped with sesame seeds and sides of sweet and sour sauce and cucumber achaar.

Mom's Chicken Wontons

Makes 38 wontons

For Asian American kids, and people foraying into Thai food for the first time, the chicken wonton is kind of our version of the chicken nugget. This was a very introductory dish for a lot of people's children when they were first coming out to International Market. Because it's such a crowd-pleaser, my mom would always prepare these for school functions, birthday parties, and fundraisers. I even remember one summer when there was a food festival our family participated in. While all the other chefs were preparing bougie recipes, my mom competed with these. I can't remember if she won, but I can wholeheartedly say these fried wontons are winners. Bonus: The filling for these wontons also works great in dumplings and atop savory toasts, and you can just as easily use pork instead.

For the filling:

- 8 ounces (225 g) ground chicken thigh (see Note)
- ½ cup (100 g) finely chopped bamboo shoots, prepared per the instructions on page 18
- 2 tablespoons finely chopped white onion
- 1 teaspoon garlic powder
- 1½ teaspoons oyster sauce
- 1 tablespoon finely chopped fresh cilantro
- 1 large egg
- 1 teaspoon Magic Powder (aka Asian chicken bouillon)

For the wontons:

- 1 (14-ounce / 400 g) package store-bought wonton wrappers, thawed if frozen
- 1 egg yolk, whisked
- Neutral oil, such as sunflower, for frying (about 6 cups / 1.4 liters)
- International Market OG Sweet and Sour Sauce (page 57), for serving

MAKE THE FILLING:

In a medium bowl, combine the chicken, bamboo shoots, onion, garlic powder, oyster sauce, cilantro, egg, and magic powder.

MAKE THE WONTONS:

Place 1 teaspoon of the chicken mixture in the center of a wonton wrapper. Using your finger or a small brush, coat the edges with egg yolk. Carefully fold one edge of the wrapper over the other to seal it, forming a triangle. Repeat with the remaining filling and wrappers.

Pour the oil to come 1 inch (2.5 cm) up the sides of a large pot and heat over medium heat until the oil reaches 325°F (165°C) when measured with a deep-fry thermometer.

Working in batches, fry the wontons in the hot oil, leaving plenty of room for the wontons to dance, until golden and cooked through, 3 to 5 minutes. Using a spider or slotted spoon, remove and drain the wontons on a paper towel–lined plate.

Serve immediately with sweet and sour sauce for dipping.

Note: If you can't find ground chicken thigh, you can pulse boneless chicken thighs in the food processor until ground.

Khanom Jeeb

Yai's Pork Shumai Dumplings

Makes 26 to 28 dumplings

If I had to select one dish to uphold my yai (my grandmother's) legacy, it would be these succulent steamed dumplings. It is inspired by the Chinese migrants in Thailand, so many of whom call Bangkok home. The recipe has remained the same for decades, a harmonious blend of ground pork, crunchy water chestnuts, and plump shrimp. I've folded these dumplings hundreds of times and have never found a single fault in them. I hold this dish especially close to my heart because the last conversation I had with my mother before she passed away revolved around this very recipe. She told me, "Honey, don't ever change this recipe. It's perfect . . . be good. I love you."

For the dumplings:

2 large eggs

1 pound (455 g) ground pork

8 ounces (225 g) large shrimp, shelled, deveined, and finely chopped (see Note)

¼ cup (35 g) finely chopped white onion

¼ cup (45 g) finely chopped water chestnuts

¼ cup (40 g) finely chopped scallions (about 3 scallions)

2 tablespoons fish sauce

2 tablespoons oyster sauce

1 tablespoon finely chopped garlic

1 teaspoon sugar

1 teaspoon kosher salt

1 teaspoon ground white pepper

2 tablespoons cornstarch

Neutral oil, such as sunflower, for the steamer basket

26 to 28 Dumpling Skins (page 46) or store-bought gyoza wrappers, thawed if frozen

For serving:

Sliced scallions, green parts only

Fried Garlic (page 65), or store-bought fried garlic

Pickled onions (optional)

Dumpling Sauce (page 58)

MAKE THE DUMPLINGS:

In a large bowl, whisk the eggs and then add the pork, shrimp, onion, water chestnuts, scallions, fish sauce, oyster sauce, garlic, sugar, salt, and white pepper and stir combine. Evenly sprinkle the cornstarch over the top and stir. If not using immediately, cover and refrigerate for up to 2 days.

Pour water to come 1 inch (2.5 cm) up the sides of a saucepan large enough to fit a steamer basket and bring to a boil over high heat. Coat a steamer basket with oil. Lay 6 wrappers on a clean work surface, keeping the remaining wrappers covered with a damp kitchen or paper towel. Place 1 heaping tablespoon of the mixture in the center of a wrapper. Fold the sides of the wrapper around the mixture, leaving the top of the dumpling open with the mixture exposed. Put the dumplings in the prepared steamer basket without touching. Repeat with the remaining filling.

Place the steamer basket above the boiling water, making sure the water doesn't touch the dumplings. Lower the heat to maintain a simmer and cook the dumplings until the pork is cooked through to 145°F (63°C) when measured with an instant-read thermometer), 8 to 10 minutes.

TO SERVE:

Serve the dumplings immediately, topped with scallions, fried garlic and/or pickled onions, if using, and dumpling sauce. Store leftovers in an airtight container in the refrigerator for up to 3 days or freeze in a single layer in a zip-top bag and re-steam from frozen.

COLD SNACK

Tod Mahn
Seafood Fritters

Makes 15 (2-ounce / 55 g) fritters

I know people love their orders of egg rolls and dumplings, but if I had to pick an appetizer that feels definitively Thai, it'd be tod mahn. These tiny patties are very versatile because they can be made with fish or shrimp and often incorporate a red curry paste, making them savory, herbaceous, and a little bit spicy. You blitz the fish, shrimp, egg, and aromatics together and fold in chopped long beans, which add a nice nuttiness and texture. The trickiest part about getting tod mahn right is making sure everything is incorporated without the texture becoming too gluey, so be careful not to overprocess the meat in the food processor. But once you spoon these fritters into the pan and fry them off, it's hard to find fault with them.

1 pound (455 g) cod or other firm-fleshed white fish fillet, skin removed

1 pound (455 g) large whole shrimp, shelled and deveined

2 tablespoons red curry paste

2 tablespoons fish sauce

2 tablespoons rice flour

1 tablespoon Magic Powder (aka Asian chicken bouillon)

1 tablespoon sugar

1 tablespoon baking powder

1 tablespoon finely chopped garlic

8 ounces (225 g) chopped shrimp

1 tablespoon thinly sliced fresh makrut lime leaves (ribs removed)

1 tablespoon chopped fresh dill

4 ounces (115 g) green beans, thinly sliced (1 cup sliced)

1 tablespoon neutral oil, such as sunflower, plus additional for frying (about 6 cups / 1.4 liters)

For serving:

Crushed roasted, unsalted peanuts

Fresh cilantro leaves

Sauce Gai (Sweet Chile Sauce, page 60)

In a food processor, combine the fish, whole shrimp, red curry paste, fish sauce, rice flour, magic powder, sugar, baking powder, and garlic and pulse to a paste-like consistency. Transfer the mixture to a medium bowl. Using a rubber spatula, fold in the chopped shrimp, lime leaves, dill, and green beans and drizzle the 1 tablespoon oil into the mixture.

Pour oil to come 1½ inches (4 cm) up the sides of a large pot and heat over medium heat until the oil reaches 325°F (165°C) when measured with a deep-fry thermometer.

Using a 2-ounce (60 ml) ice cream scoop or ¼ cup measuring cup, measure out 2-ounce (60 ml) portions of the mixture and place them on a baking pan. Roll the portions into 2-inch (5 cm) balls and press to flatten them slightly to form patties. To prevent the fritters from puffing up, make a small indention with your thumb in the center of each patty.

Carefully fry the patties, making sure not to overcrowd the pan. The fritters will slowly float to the surface as they cook, after about 30 seconds. Flip and cook the other side until golden brown, 1 to 2 minutes. Remove the patties and transfer to a wire cooling rack or paper towel–lined plate to remove any excess oil. Return the oil to 325°F (165°C) if the temperature has dropped and fry the remaining fritters in batches.

TO SERVE:

Serve immediately topped with crushed peanuts, cilantro, and a side of sauce gai, or keep warm on an oven-safe platter in a preheated 200°F (90°C) oven until ready to serve.

Thai Street Corn

Serves 6

A cup of corn tossed in a very curiously yellow butter with a sprinkle of sugar and salt is a fond memory from my trips to night markets during my vacations to Thailand when I was a kid. And who doesn't love the Mexican street corn elote? We Thais needed our own version. I've taken the concept and flavor profiles of elote and Thai-ed them up using some accessible pantry ingredients. My coconut red curry butter offers a fresh take on this street snack favorite. To make the corn even better, soak it in a warm water brine of salt and sugar before preparing it so the flavor can really penetrate between each kernel. Trust me, it makes a difference.

For the corn:

- 3 quarts (2.8 liters) warm water
- 3 tablespoons sugar
- 4 teaspoons kosher salt
- 6 medium ears corn, husks and silks removed
- 1 tablespoon neutral oil, such as sunflower

For the red curry butter:

- 1 tablespoon red curry paste
- 1 tablespoon coconut milk
- 1 cup (2 sticks / 225 g) unsalted butter, at room temperature
- 4 fresh cilantro springs, leaves and stems, chopped
- 1 teaspoon sugar
- ½ teaspoon kosher salt

For serving:

- 2 scallions, green and white parts, thinly sliced
- 1 teaspoon Prik Pohn (Toasted Ground Chile, page 54) or crushed dried Thai chile (about 2 chiles)
- 1 tablespoon sweetened coconut flakes
- Thinly sliced Fresno chiles
- Popcorn
- 2 limes, cut into cheeks (see page 50)

BRINE THE CORN:

Pour the water into a large stockpot and add the sugar and salt. Add the corn, place a plate on top to keep the corn submerged, and allow the ears to soak in the refrigerator for at least 12 hours up to 24 hours.

Remove the corn from the brine and pat dry with paper towels.

MAKE THE RED CURRY BUTTER:

In a medium bowl, whisk the red curry paste and coconut milk. Stir in the butter, cilantro, sugar, and salt. If you're not using it immediately, cover and refrigerate until 30 minutes before use (you want the butter to be soft and spreadable, not melted).

COOK THE CORN:

Adjust a rack 5 to 6 inches (12 to 15 cm) from your oven's heat source and preheat the broiler to high.

Lightly coat the corn with the oil and place it on a baking pan in a single layer. Broil until the corn begins to brown and char, about 4 minutes. Carefully rotate the corn and continue to broil until browned all over, about another 4 minutes. Remove and, using a towel to hold the corn, slice the ears into 1-inch (2.5 cm) pieces and transfer to a serving platter.

TO SERVE:

Dollop the pieces with the red curry butter and sprinkle with the scallions, prik pohn, coconut, Fresno chiles, and popcorn. Serve immediately with lime cheeks on the side.

Miang Khao Tod
Red Curry Fried Rice Balls

Serves 6

This is my vegetarian take on a traditional rice ball salad from Northeastern Thailand that typically calls for sour fermented pork. You still get all those tart flavors and subtle curry heat, but without meat. The magic of miang khao tod is all in the texture: The rice becomes irresistibly crunchy once shaped into baseball-size spheres and deep fried, like a spicy, fragrant version of arancini. Cracking the rice balls open and serving them with peanuts, cilantro, and red onions all wrapped in lettuce leaves makes for the perfect bite.

- ¼ cup (30 g) sweet shredded coconut
- Neutral oil, such as sunflower, for frying (about 4 quarts / 4 liters)
- 2 tablespoons red curry paste
- 2 tablespoons chopped sweet preserved radish
- ¼ cup (15 g) Fried Shallots (page 64), or store-bought fried shallots
- 2 tablespoons sliced scallions, green and white parts
- 1½ tablespoons thinly sliced fresh makrut lime leaves (ribs removed)
- 1 tablespoon sugar
- 1 teaspoon MSG
- 2 cups (280 g) cooked jasmine rice, warm

For serving:

- Roasted, unsalted peanuts
- Sliced Fresno chiles
- Sliced red onion
- Fresh ginger, peeled and cut into thin strips
- Fresh mint leaves
- Lime cheeks (see page 50)
- 6 to 12 green lettuce leaves, such as green oak

In a dry medium skillet, toast the coconut over medium heat until pale golden brown, 2 to 3 minutes. Set aside.

Pour oil to come 3 inches (7.5 cm) up the sides of a large pot. Heat over medium heat until the oil reaches 325°F (165°C) when measured with a deep-fry thermometer.

In a large bowl, combine the red curry paste, preserved radish, fried shallots, toasted coconut, scallions, lime leaves, sugar, and MSG (or salt). Add the warm rice and mix to evenly combine. Using your hands or disposable gloves if the rice is hot, shape 1 cup (180 g) of the rice mixture into a tightly packed 2-inch (5 cm) ball. Use a piece of plastic wrap to fully wrap the rice ball and twist the plastic around the ball as tight as possible to make sure the rice is bound together, solid, and firm. Repeat with the remaining rice mixture to make 2 more balls.

Remove the plastic wrap from a rice ball and, using a spider or mesh strainer, gently lower it into the oil. Cook until the exterior is golden brown, 1 to 2 minutes. Remove from the oil and transfer to a paper towel–lined plate. Bring the oil back to 325°F (165°C) and fry the remaining rice balls.

Return the first rice ball to the oil and fry until crispy and browned, about 1 minute. Transfer to the paper towel–lined plate and, using another sheet of paper towel, gently press the ball to set its shape and absorb any excess oil. Repeat with remaining rice balls.

TO SERVE:

Place the rice balls on a bed of peanuts, Fresno chiles, red onion, ginger, and mint. Mash the rice balls and toss with the bed of garnishes, then squeeze lime cheeks over everything. Wrap in lettuce leaves to make 6 to 12 wraps and serve.

Watermelon Chile Crumble

Serves 4 to 6

There is an old-school style of Thai cooking known as *bolan* that dates back to ancient times. On my last visit to Thailand, I met and cooked in the home of Chef Cherwan Bunnag, a fellow Thai chef whose family lineage is connected to Thai royalty. One of the bolan dishes we made was watermelon cubes tossed with a sugary, salty crumble made from dried fish floss. It may sound strange, but trust me, this salty, sweet combo is irresistible. It sort of reminds me of the chamoy or mango with Tajín that they serve from Mexican fruit carts, although with much more umami flavor. Fish floss is traditional, but I created my own take for the restaurant using chile jam and nam prik klang dong, a crumble made from a mix of dried shrimp, anchovies, and fried shallots. It mirrors the original's textural experience and is just as full of exciting flavors. The savory crumble, the spicy sauce, and the fragrant herbs will show you how versatile watermelon can be.

12 (½-inch / 12 mm thick) watermelon wedges (from 1 small, seedless watermelon; about 4 pounds / 1.8 kg)

¼ cup (70 g) nam prik pao (roasted chile jam)

1 cup (80 g) Nam Prik Klang Dong (Caramelized Dried Shrimp and Anchovy Crumble, page 76)

1 stalk lemongrass (about 1 ounce / 25 g), ends trimmed, tough outer layers removed, and thinly sliced

24 fresh mint leaves

12 fresh cilantro leaves

Arrange the watermelon wedges on a serving platter (in the restaurant, I like to shingle them, so the edges are overlapping). Spoon the nam prik pao over the watermelon. Sprinkle the nam prik klang dong evenly over the wedges and garnish with the lemongrass, mint, and cilantro. Serve immediately.

CHILE
JAM

Son-in-Law Eggs
Deep-Fried Boiled Eggs

Makes 6 eggs

It's debated why son-in-law eggs are called son-in-law eggs. I won't get into the gritty—and perhaps shocking?—details, but I'm sure you can use your imagination! However strange the name is, don't let it dissuade you from making this dish. Simple boiled eggs are fried and dressed in a sticky salty-sweet tamarind sauce. The whites of the egg get a crispy outer shell, while the yolks remain delightfully creamy. When you add fried shallots, cilantro, and makrut lime leaves, it makes for a memorable bite.

For the sauce:

1 tablespoon neutral oil, such as sunflower

1 shallot (2 ounces / 56 g), thinly sliced into rounds

8 whole dried Thai chiles

2 (2-ounce / 55 g) disks palm sugar

¼ cup (115 g) tamarind concentrate

¼ cup (60 ml) fish sauce

2 tablespoons of vinegar from Pickled Garlic and Vinegar (page 62)

For the eggs:

Neutral oil, such as sunflower, for frying (about 6 cups / 1.4 L)

6 large eggs, at room temperature

Ice, as needed

For serving:

¼ cup Fried Shallots (page 64), or store-bought fried shallots

12 fresh cilantro leaves

Thinly sliced makrut lime leaves, ribs removed

MAKE THE SAUCE:

Put the oil and shallots in a small saucepan and cook over medium heat until slightly browned, about 3 minutes. Add the Thai chiles, palm sugar, tamarind concentrate, fish sauce, pickled garlic vinegar, and ¼ cup (60 ml) water. Bring to a simmer and simmer to dissolve the sugar and cook out the acidity of the vinegar (the consistency should be similar to pancake syrup), about 10 minutes.

MAKE THE EGGS:

Pour oil to come 1 inch (2.5 cm) up the sides of a deep, wide saucepan or Dutch oven. Heat over medium heat to 325°F (165°C).

Fill a medium saucepan with enough water to cover the eggs by 1 inch (2.5 cm) and bring to a boil over high heat.

Using a spider or slotted spoon, gently place the eggs into the water and cook for 6 minutes.

Meanwhile, fill a large bowl with ice and cold water to make an ice bath. Remove the eggs and immediately transfer to the ice bath. Tap ends of the eggs against one another to slightly crack the shells and return to the ice bath to cool completely. Peel the eggs and pat dry with paper towels to remove any excess water.

Using a dry spider or slotted spoon, gently lower the dry peeled eggs into the hot oil and cook until the outer white of the eggs starts to brown and crisp, 3 to 5 minutes. Do not overcrowd the pot to ensure even cooking; cook in batches if necessary. Remove the eggs and transfer to a paper towel–lined plate to remove excess oil.

TO SERVE:

Slice the fried, boiled eggs in half and arrange on a plate. Generously drizzle with the sauce, spooning some of the cooked shallots and Thai chiles on top of the eggs. Garnish with fried shallots, cilantro, and lime leaves.

Sakoo Sai Moo

Tapioca Pork Dumplings with Caramelized Radish and Peanut

Makes 40 dumplings

Sakoo sai moo is one of the prettiest appetizers and nostalgically craveable street snacks from my childhood. These tapioca dumplings, often colored in soft lavender shades thanks to butterfly pea flowers, look like shiny pearls. They have a chewy, mochi-like exterior that gives way to a sweet and salty pork filling that's packed with preserved radish, garlic, and ground peanuts. These dumplings are then finished with fried garlic and served with a side of Thai chiles and lettuce leaves. They're almost *too* pretty to eat, but once you catch a whiff of that peppery pork filling, nothing can hold you back.

For the tapioca dumplings:

2 cups (340 g) small tapioca pearls

Nonstick cooking spray

For the pork filling:

¼ cup (60 ml) neutral oil, such as sunflower

¼ cup (40 g) finely chopped red onion

8 ounces (225 g) ground pork

1 tablespoon finely chopped garlic

1 tablespoon chopped fresh cilantro stems

¼ cup (60 g) chopped sweet preserved radish

3 (2-ounce / 55 g) disks palm sugar

3 tablespoons thin soy sauce or Thai seasoning sauce

1½ teaspoons ground black pepper

¼ cup (53 g) finely ground peanuts

Nonstick cooking spray

Garlic Oil (page 65)

For serving:

Small Bibb or butter lettuce leaves

Fried Garlic (page 65), or store-bought fried garlic

Fresh red Thai chiles

Fresh cilantro sprigs

(Recipe continues)

MAKE THE DUMPLINGS:

Place the tapioca pearls in a medium bowl **(1)**. Cover them with 2 cups (480 ml) room-temperature water. Let stand for 10 minutes. Strain through a fine-mesh sieve and let drain for 15 minutes.

Generously spray a steamer basket with cooking spray.

MEANWHILE, MAKE THE FILLING:

In a large skillet, heat the oil over medium heat until shimmering. Add the onion and cook, stirring, until translucent, about 3 minutes. Add the pork, garlic, and cilantro stems and cook, stirring occasionally, until there is almost no pink left in the pork. Add the preserved radish, palm sugar, soy sauce, and black pepper and cook until the sugar is dissolved and the sauce is reduced, 6 to 8 minutes. Remove the mixture from the heat and fold in the peanuts. Let cool. Shape into ½-inch (12 mm) balls, about the size of a bonbon.

FINISH THE DUMPLINGS:

In the palm of your hand, shape 1 heaping tablespoon of the cooled tapioca pearls into a ball and once it becomes tacky, press it into a 1½- to 2-inch (4 to 5 cm) diameter disk **(2)**. Press a filling ball into the center of the disk and wrap the disk around the filling to seal it completely **(3)**. Using your hands, roll the filled disk into a smooth ball **(4)** and place it in the prepared steamer basket. Repeat with the remaining tapioca and filling.

Pour water into a saucepan large enough to fit a steamer basket to come 1 inch (2.5 cm) up the sides. Bring to a boil over high heat.

Reduce the heat to medium. Lightly coat the dumplings with cooking spray. Set the basket over the boiling water, cover, and cook until the tapioca is translucent, 5 to 7 minutes. Remove the steamed dumplings and transfer, a few at a time, to a medium bowl. Add some garlic oil and gently toss to coat completely. Repeat with the remaining dumplings.

TO SERVE:

Arrange the dumplings on a platter with the lettuce, fried garlic, and Thai chiles. To eat, place a dumpling into a lettuce leaf and top with fried garlic, Thai chile, and cilantro sprigs.

1
ASIAN BEST
TAPIOCA PEARLS

2

3

4

Kuah Gai Tod
Crispy Garlic Chicken Bites

Serves 4

Every day, as we prep the kitchen for service, we have scrap chicken. Instead of wasting these tiny bits of meat, we make ourselves this snack instead. You can easily make this, too, with the boneless, skinless chicken thighs that have been sitting in your freezer awaiting inspiration to strike. This dish is essentially a savory chicken nugget bite, like my Thai take on Japanese karaage. We have a bowl of this stuff during service for anyone who needs some added pep in their step. The sauce gets really caramelized in the fryer, which annoyingly turns the oil black, but the satisfying bite is worth it.

- 2 pounds (910 g) boneless, skinless chicken thighs, cut into 1-inch-thick (2.5 cm) strips (about 8)
- ¼ cup (55 g) finely chopped garlic
- ¼ cup (60 ml) oyster sauce
- 2 tablespoons Thai seasoning sauce
- 2 tablespoons sugar
- 1 teaspoon ground white pepper
- Neutral oil, such as sunflower, for frying (about 6 cups / 1.4 L)

For serving:

- Garlic Oil (page 65)
- Nam Jim Jaeow (Dried Chile Sauce, page 72)
- Sticky Rice (page 38)

In a large bowl, combine the chicken with the garlic, oyster sauce, Thai seasoning sauce, sugar, and white pepper. Let stand at room temperature for 30 minutes to marinate.

Pour enough oil to come 1 inch (2.5 cm) up the sides of a large saucepan. Heat to 325°F (165°C) when measured with a deep-fry thermometer.

Remove the chicken from the marinade and, using paper towels, pat dry to remove any excess marinade.

Working in small batches (you want plenty of room for the chicken pieces to move in the oil), gently add the marinated chicken to the hot oil and fry until the chicken is opaque, about 1½ minutes. Using a spider or metal slotted spoon, carefully remove them from the oil, transfer to a wire cooling rack, and let rest for 3 minutes. Bring the oil back to 325°F (165°C) and fry the remaining chicken.

After resting, return the chicken, again in batches, to the 325°F (165° C) oil and fry until browned and cooked through (with an internal temperature of 165°F (75°C) when measured with an instant-read thermometer), 2 to 3 minutes (see Note).

TO SERVE:

In a large bowl, toss the fried chicken with a generous tablespoon or two of garlic oil (if you get some of the garlic bits in there, even better!). Serve warm with nam jim jaeow and sticky rice.

Note: If you don't wish to fry the chicken a second time, you can finish cooking the chicken in a preheated 350°F (175°C) oven until cooked through, about 5 minutes.

RANKIN DELUX

Nuah Daad Diew
Beef Jerky

Makes 1 pound; serves 4

You know how beef jerky is a kind of road trip food in America? The same goes in Thailand. Everyone's Thai grandma knows to pack some jerky and sticky rice for a long travel day, wrapped in foil and kept warm. Unlike your standard jerky that really works your jaw muscles, Thai jerky has a tenderness that makes it easy to devour. It's savory thanks to a combination of Magic Powder and oyster sauce, and when you eat it with a ball of sticky rice, it's a match made in heaven. I know that someday I'll be packing a road trip snack or two for my daughter that includes this jerky and rice. In the meantime, however, I'll keep preparing and eating this fresh, no road trip necessary.

- 2 tablespoons oyster sauce
- 2 tablespoons sugar
- 2 tablespoons Thai seasoning sauce
- 1 tablespoon finely chopped garlic
- 2 teaspoons Magic Powder (aka Asian chicken bouillon)
- ½ teaspoon Chinese five-spice powder
- ½ teaspoon ground white pepper
- ½ teaspoon kosher salt
- 1 pound (455 g) top sirloin or chuck steak, 2 inches (5 cm) thick, trimmed and thinly sliced
- Neutral oil, such as sunflower, for frying (about 8 cups / 1 L)

For serving:

- Fried Shallots (page 64), or store-bought fried shallots
- Cabbage wedges
- Prik Pohn (Toasted Ground Chile, page 54)
- Fresh red Thai chiles
- Nam Jim Jaeow (Dried Chile Sauce, page 72)
- Sticky Rice (page 38)

In a large zip-top bag, combine the oyster sauce, sugar, seasoning sauce, garlic, magic powder, five-spice powder, white pepper, and salt. Add the beef slices and shake to thoroughly coat. Seal the bag, pressing out as much air as possible, and refrigerate for at least 2 hours and up to 24 hours to marinate.

Preheat the oven to 250°F (120°C).

Place the marinated beef on a baking pan fitted with a wired rack in an even layer. Bake until the exterior is just slightly moist and bendable, about 2 hours. Remove the pan from the oven and let cool completely.

Pour enough oil to come 1 inch (2.5 cm) up the sides of a large saucepan. Heat over medium heat to 325°F (165°C) when measured with a deep-fry thermometer. Gently place the cooled beef, a few pieces at a time, into the hot oil and fry until slightly crisp, 1 to 3 minutes. Remove the slices from the oil and transfer to a wire rack. Fry the remaining beef.

TO SERVE:

Garnish the jerky with fried shallots and serve it warm with cabbage wedges, prik pohn, Thai chiles, sticky rice, and a small dish of nam jim jaeow for dipping, or cover and refrigerate for up to 5 days.

To reheat the jerky, place the slices on a baking pan and broil in the oven or toaster oven. It's OK to eat it cold as well, just not as fabulous. Serve it with nam jim jaeow and sticky rice.

Gai Yang
Bangkok BBQ Chicken

Serves 4

If there's something that's quintessentially Thailand, it's the smell of bamboo-speared chicken grilling over hot coals on the side of a road. Juicy, tender chicken hidden beneath caramelized chicken skin and gorgeous grill marks is hard to beat, but I don't always feel like going outside to grill. That's why I developed this recipe: to achieve the essence of gai yang without coals. My recipe may not be as traditional as the roadside version, but it does satisfy any cravings for classic Thai street food flavors. Serving this with sweet chile sauce and a side of sticky rice is mandatory.

- 1 tablespoon oyster sauce
- 1 tablespoon chopped garlic
- 1 tablespoon sugar
- 1½ teaspoons Madras curry powder
- 1½ teaspoons Magic Powder (aka Asian chicken bouillon)
- 1 teaspoon Chinese five-spice powder
- 1 teaspoon kosher salt
- 2 pounds (910 g) skinless, boneless chicken thighs (about 8)

For serving:

- Fresh cilantro leaves
- Sticky Rice (page 38)
- Sauce Gai (Sweet Chile Sauce, page 60)
- Cucumber Achaar (page 196; optional)

In a large zip-top bag, combine the oyster sauce, garlic, sugar, curry powder, magic powder, five-spice powder, and salt. Add the chicken thighs and rub to thoroughly coat. Seal the bag, pressing out as much air as possible, and marinate in the refrigerator for at least 1 hour or up to 4 hours.

Preheat the oven to 400°F (205°C).

Remove the chicken from the marinade and, using paper towels, pat dry. Place the marinated chicken thighs on a baking pan in a single layer. Bake the chicken until it reaches an internal temperature of 145°F (65°C) on an oven-safe thermometer, 13 to 15 minutes. Adjust the oven control to broil and move the baking pan 5 to 6 inches from the heat source. Broil until the chicken is slightly charred and cooked to an internal temperature of 165°F (75°C), about 5 minutes more.

TO SERVE:

Transfer to a platter and garnish with cilantro. Serve with sticky rice, sauce gai, and cucumber achaar, if using.

Laab Tod
Spicy Pork Meatballs

Makes 18 meatballs

Frying laab, the herbaceous minced meat Thai salad (see page 210), into little meatballs adds a new and crunchy dimension. It's still got all the best parts of laab that you love, like plenty of lime juice and toasted rice powder (which you already know how to make thanks to the recipe on page 65), but with an added sear. You can eat these meatballs whole, over a bed of rice, or break them up and put them in lettuce wraps for a refreshing appetizer. For added heat, serve with a side of nam jim jaeow.

For the meatballs:

2 pounds (910 g) ground pork

¼ cup (35 g) finely chopped white onion

¼ cup (20 g) chopped fresh cilantro stems and leaves

3 tablespoons finely chopped lemongrass (from about 1½ stalks)

2 tablespoons finely chopped fresh makrut lime leaves (ribs removed; 12 leaves)

1 tablespoon fresh lime juice

1 tablespoon fine rice flour

1 tablespoon Khao Kuah (Toasted Rice Powder, page 62)

1 tablespoon Prik Pohn (Toasted Ground Chile, page 54)

1½ teaspoons fish sauce

1½ teaspoons sugar

1½ teaspoons Magic Powder (aka Asian chicken bouillon) or MSG

1½ teaspoons kosher salt

Neutral oil, such as sunflower, for frying (about 8 cups / 2 L)

For serving:

Thinly sliced red onion

Fresh cilantro leaves

Cabbage wedges

Nam Jim Jaeow (Dried Chile Sauce, page 72)

MAKE THE MEATBALLS:

Preheat the oven to 350°F (175°C).

In a large bowl, combine the pork, onion, cilantro, lemongrass, lime leaves, lime juice, rice flour, khao kuah, prik pohn, fish sauce, sugar, magic powder, and salt. Mix until evenly incorporated and let stand for 15 minutes.

Using a 1½-ounce (45 ml) ice-cream scoop, shape the meatballs into tightly pressed balls about 2 inches (5 cm) in diameter by rolling them with your hands. Place on a baking pan with space between them.

Pour oil to come about 2 inches (5 cm) up the sides of a medium saucepan (enough to submerge the meatballs). Heat over medium heat to 325°F (165°C) when measured with a deep-fry thermometer. Gently place a few meatballs into the hot oil, being careful not to overcrowd the pan. Cook the meatballs, turning occasionally, until the exterior turns brown and becomes slightly crispy, about 2 minutes; remove and transfer to a clean baking pan. Repeat with the remaining meatballs.

Bake the meatballs until the internal temperature reaches 165°F (75°C) when measured with an instant-read thermometer, about 10 minutes.

TO SERVE:

Place the warm meatballs in a bowl on a platter. Garnish with red onion and serve with cilantro, cabbage wedges, and a ramekin of nam jim jaeow. Or refrigerate the meatballs in an airtight container for up to 3 days and reheat before serving.

CLOCKWISE FROM TOP:
Nuah Daad Diew (page 110),
Laab Tod (page opposite),
Gai Yang (page 111).

Tofu Dang
Char Siu Tofu

Serves 4

This is one of the recipes I'm most proud of. If you've ever had char siu, or Chinese-style barbecue pork, you know how juicy, sweet, and striking it can be. The hue is an eye-catching red and the pork typically glistens with rendered fat. It's harder to achieve that same texture with tofu, yet I've invented something that's even better. The smokiness of the barbecue is still there, as well as the recognizable red color and the gentle sweetness. I also press the tofu to ensure the texture has bite. Although the fat of a cut of pork shoulder can't be replaced, with this tofu version, you won't even miss it. Everyone, vegetarians and non-vegetarians alike, will cheer for this dish.

2 tablespoons ketchup
2 tablespoons brown sugar
2 tablespoons finely chopped garlic
2 teaspoons hoisin sauce
1 teaspoon Thai seasoning sauce
1 teaspoon black soy sauce
1 teaspoon kosher salt
⅛ teaspoon Chinese five-spice powder
⅛ teaspoon ground white pepper
3 drops red food coloring
2 (6.5-ounce / 184 g) packages tofu cutlet, pressed tofu, or unflavored baked tofu
Thinly sliced scallions, green parts only, for serving

In a medium bowl, combine the ketchup, brown sugar, garlic, hoisin sauce, Thai seasoning sauce, soy sauce, salt, five-spice powder, white pepper, and red food coloring. Set aside.

With paper towels, pat the tofu dry. Using a bamboo skewer or fork, generously but gently pierce the tofu blocks all over the top, bottom, and sides. Fully coat the pierced tofu blocks with the ketchup mixture and place in an airtight container. Cover and marinate in the refrigerator for at least 4 days and up to 6 days.

Preheat the oven to 350°F (175°C).

Remove the tofu from the marinade, reserving any leftover marinade, and transfer to a baking pan. Bake the tofu, brushing with the marinade several times during cooking, about 20 minutes. Switch the oven to broil and broil the tofu on one side for 2 minutes, or until you achieve a BBQ-like char.

Serve immediately, drizzled with the leftover marinade if desired, and garnished with scallions. Store leftovers in the refrigerator in an airtight container for up to 5 days and thinly slice to eat cold or reheat as desired.

Haw Mok
Steamed Red Curry Fish Custard

Makes 6 custards

For me, haw mok is proof that many different flavor profiles can find harmony and unison in a single dish. The coconut cream tames the brine of the fish sauce and the heat from the curry paste. The addition of cabbage and fish make these custards hearty yet light. Makrut lime leaves add a hint of citrus without acid, and the steamed banana leaf, a traditional method of wrapping haw mok into a parcel, infuses an earthy fragrance. For this recipe, we'll be using ramekins alongside the banana leaves so the haw mok can hold its shape better. You can think of this as a savory red curry custard, or perhaps a spicy Thai tamale.

For the custard:

1 pound (455 g) white fish, such as cod or whiting

2 large eggs

3 tablespoons red curry paste

1 tablespoon fish sauce

2 cups (480 ml) coconut milk

1 tablespoon sugar

1 teaspoon thinly sliced makrut lime leaves (ribs removed), plus more for serving

1 to 2 banana leaves, cut into 12 rectangles that fit your ramekins

1 cup (80 g) thinly sliced green cabbage

12 fresh Thai basil leaves

For the coconut glaze:

1 cup (240 ml) coconut cream

2 tablespoons rice flour

For serving:

Thinly sliced fresh red Thai chiles

Fresh cilantro leaves

Thinly sliced makrut lime leaves

MAKE THE CUSTARD:

Pour water into a saucepan large enough to fit a steamer basket to come 1 inch (2.5 cm) up the sides. Bring to a boil over high heat.

In a food processor, pulse half of the fish until very smooth. Roughly chop the remaining fish by hand and set aside.

In a large bowl, combine eggs, red curry paste, fish sauce, coconut milk, sugar, and lime leaves. Fold in the processed fish and chopped fish until evenly combined. You'll have about 3 cups (720 ml). Set aside.

Line the bottom of 6 (6- to 8-ounce / 180 to 240 ml) oven-safe ramekins with two banana leaves, criss-crossed and coming up the sides (but not hanging over). Cover the banana leaves with a thin layer of cabbage and Thai basil leaves. Ladle the fish custard mixture evenly into each ramekin, filling to within ¼ inch (6 mm) from the top.

Reduce the heat to medium-low. Transfer the ramekins into a steamer basket and place the steamer basket over the saucepan. Cover and steam the custards, maintaining a rolling simmer, until fully set and a toothpick inserted comes out clean, 20 to 25 minutes. Turn off the heat and let the custards set for 2 minutes.

MEANWHILE, MAKE THE COCONUT CREAM GLAZE:

In a small saucepan, combine the coconut cream and rice flour and whisk with a wire whisk over medium heat until thick, about 2 minutes. Cool the coconut glaze.

TO SERVE:

Dollop the coconut glaze on top of each cooked custard, garnish with Thai chiles, cilantro, and lime leaves, and serve immediately.

Hoy Tod
Mussel and Bean Sprout Pancake

Makes 2 omelets; serves 2 to 4

Hoy tod is the sister dish to pad Thai, and those who know, know. This dish is classic Bangkok street food at its best, a true and dynamic definition of Thai street food for Thai people. The recipe begins with plump mussels. A runny rice flour batter is poured over the shellfish and spread thin so that it immediately crisps up over a hot, well-oiled wok. The edges of this pancake and omelet hybrid become super crunchy while the center is filled with softened bean sprouts. The batter also has a slightly chewier bite thanks to the mochi-like rice flour. I love the textural landscape of this seafood omelet. And just when you think it can't get any better, you drizzle it with my homemade hot sauce and experience street food euphoria from home.

For the sauce:

¼ cup (60 ml) Sriracha (page 60), or store-bought sriracha

¼ cup (60 ml) Sauce Gai (Sweet Chile Sauce, page 60)

2 tablespoons distilled white vinegar

For the mussels:

1 pound (455 g) mussels (or 8 ounces / 225 g cooked mussel meat), scrubbed and debearded (see Note)

For the pancake batter:

¼ cup (40 g) tapioca starch

1 tablespoon rice flour

1 teaspoon baking powder

½ cup (120 ml) lemon lime soda, such as Sprite

Pinch of kosher salt

Pinch of ground white pepper

2 scallions, green and white parts, thinly sliced

For the filling:

Neutral oil, such as sunflower

2 large eggs

1 tablespoon chopped garlic

4 ounces (115 g) bean sprouts (2 cups)

2 splashes of fish sauce

For serving:

Fresh cilantro leaves

Note: Run your mussels under cold water and scrub them to get rid of any mud or seaweed on their outer shells. Tap the mussels on the counter to make sure they are sealed tight. Press together the shells of any that are open. If the shell doesn't stay closed, the mussel is dead and should be discarded (also toss any with broken shells). Most mussels are sold debearded, but check for any seaweed-like threads sticking out of the shell that remain and remove them by pulling on them firmly and discarding them.

(Recipe continues)

RECYCLE
ME

MAKE THE SAUCE:

In a medium bowl, combine the sriracha, sauce gai, and vinegar. Set aside.

MAKE THE MUSSELS:

Fill a large saucepan with water to come two-thirds of the way up. Place over high heat and bring to a boil. Add the mussels and cook until the shells open, about 4 minutes. Drain and remove the meat from the shells, discarding any mussels that do not open. Refrigerate until you're ready to make the pancakes.

MAKE THE PANCAKE BATTER:

In a large bowl or glass measuring cup, combine the tapioca starch, rice flour, baking powder, soda, salt, and white pepper. Add the scallions to the batter and whisk to combine **(1)**.

MAKE THE FILLING:

In a 10-inch (25 cm) nonstick skillet, heat 1 tablespoon oil over medium-high heat until shimmering.

Pour in half of the batter, enough to coat the surface of the pan **(2)**, and cook until it begins to bubble and crisp, about 2 minutes. Using a rubber spatula, gently swirl to keep the pancake batter moving around in the skillet and prevent sticking. Evenly distribute half the mussels on top of the pancake.

Gently crack an egg directly into the center of the pancake **(3)**, break the yolk, and let it glaze the pancake **(4)**.

Using the spatula, carefully flip the pancake **(5)** and push it to one side of the skillet.

While the other side of the pancake is cooking, add half of the garlic to the empty side of the pan and cook for 30 seconds, then add half of the bean sprouts and a splash of fish sauce and stir to combine. Place the pancake on top of the garlic and sprouts **(6)** and transfer to a plate.

Repeat with the remaining batter, egg, garlic, bean sprouts, and fish sauce.

TO SERVE:

Garnish each pancake with cilantro and serve immediately with a side of the sauce.

1
2
3
4
5
6

As a chef, I could be preparing interesting gastriques or assembling elaborate desserts with tweezers, but nothing feels quite as cheffy to me as when I'm behind that wok, bursts of flame emitting from an intensely hot and unapologetic station. It's truly badass. Gleen kratat, or what's known as the wok aroma in Thai (and also called wok hei in Chinese cuisine), is such an instrumental part of the flavor of wok-cooked dishes. This style of cooking, however, is extremely hard to achieve at home (unless you're one of those lucky people who have wok setups in your backyard). The reason for that is that you need ventilation and space to have large flames leap up under your wok. In a regular home kitchen, it's hard to undertake wok cooking because the standard kitchen stovetops rarely get hot enough to fire up a wok like a restaurant kitchen. Electric and induction stovetops are even more difficult. So, although it's fun to cook in a wok and work your wrists, it's not always the best pan to use for some of the dishes in this chapter. Woks have a lot of depth, and when they don't get hot enough, sauce tends to pool at the bottom and cause a dish to steam rather than condensing and glazing a dish. I don't want you to have a soupy pad see eiw (page 135); I want your noodles, instead, to be coated in a luscious, sticky sauce and even a little char. How do we solve this problem? By using a flat-bottomed sauté pan, a stainless-steel skillet, or a cast-iron pan that can get extremely hot, heats evenly, and retains a high temperature level. And don't worry; all the recipes in my wok chapter were written with the home chef in mind, so you'll still be able to achieve beautiful dishes (and keep your eyebrows from singeing off).

Just Fork It and Eat

If I had a dollar for every time a customer at the restaurant asked me for a pair of chopsticks to eat their drunken noodles or pad see ew, I'd be incredibly wealthy. I can understand this line of thinking—chopsticks are standard utensils in other Asian countries, so one might assume Thais use chopsticks, too. I also can tell that there is an eagerness to learn and try to enjoy the meal in the most authentic possible way. I appreciate the enthusiasm, but the truth is, Thailand is a fork and spoon country (or, better yet, a hands country).

Forks and spoons were introduced to what was then the Kingdom of Siam back in the eighteenth century. Prior to that, most Thais (or, I guess, Siamese back then) ate using their hands, which is still common in Thailand, especially when it comes to sticky rice. Once the spoons and forks arrived, we never looked back.

The spoon goes into your dominant hand and the fork in the other. Whether you're eating fried rice, stir-fried noodles, or even papaya salad, you use the backside of the fork to push the food onto the spoon, before launching the spoon directly into your mouth. It is *much*, much easier to eat rice with a spoon and a fork than chopsticks—plus, you can prepare a perfect bite.

That's not to say that chopsticks are completely nonexistent in Thailand. Thailand has a lot of Chinese influence, so you'll still find chopsticks at the Chinese restaurants in Yaowarat, Bangkok's Chinatown, or when eating noodle soups like boat noodles or kuay tiew tom yum. For most of the dishes in this book, however, a spoon and a fork—or even your bare hands—are all you need.

Khao Pad
Mom's Classic Thai Fried Rice

Serves 2 to 4

What's not to love about fried rice? It's one of those dishes that's perfect for clearing out your fridge and it takes less than ten minutes to throw it all together. You can use whatever protein you want—some favorites are shrimp, crab, and thinly sliced pork, but if you want to go full vegetarian, tofu and vegetables are great options, too. Classic Thai fried rice has to have tomatoes, which provide an acidic hit; thinly sliced onions that are cooked until translucent and soft; and a pinch of Magic Powder (aka chicken bouillon powder). To spruce it up further, I love to add preserved radish, which melts into the ingredients and provides a subtle sweetness that bolsters the other flavors of this dish. It's simple food, but don't let that fool you—you'll be coming back to this recipe again and again.

¼ cup (60 ml) neutral oil, such as sunflower

1 large egg

4 ounces (115 g) large shrimp, shelled and deveined

½ cup (55 g) sliced white onion

½ cup (25 g) sliced gai lan (Chinese broccoli), leaves and stems

1 tablespoon chopped sweet preserved radish

1 tablespoon finely chopped garlic

2 cups (280 g) day-old steamed rice

1 Roma tomato (about 5½ ounces / 155 g), cut into 8 wedges

1 scallion, green and white parts, cut into 1-inch (2.5 cm) pieces

2 tablespoons Thai seasoning sauce

1 teaspoon sugar

1 teaspoon Magic Powder (aka Asian chicken bouillon)

½ teaspoon ground white pepper

For serving:

Sliced cucumber

Lime cheeks (see page 50)

Prik Nam Pla (Chile Fish Sauce, page 56)

In a large skillet, heat the oil over medium-high heat until it shimmers. Crack the egg into the oil and allow the white to coagulate, about 30 seconds. Using a flat spatula, break the egg yolk and lightly scramble the egg until it is fully cooked. Push the cooked egg to one side of the pan.

Add the shrimp and onion and cook, stirring occasionally, until the shrimp just begins to turn opaque, about 45 seconds. Add the gai lan, preserved radish, and garlic and cook, stirring, until the broccoli lightly wilts, about another 45 seconds. Add the rice, breaking up any large clumps, and fold the egg back into the mixture, along with the tomatoes and scallions. Stir in the seasoning sauce, sugar, magic powder, and white pepper and continue cooking until the rice is hot and the shrimp is fully cooked, about another 2 minutes.

TO SERVE:

Transfer the rice into a large serving bowl and gently press down to lightly pack the rice. Place a plate on top of the bowl, flip the plate and bowl together so the plate ends up on your work surface, and remove the bowl to create a dome of rice. Serve with cucumber slices, lime cheeks, and prik nam pla. Store any leftover rice in an airtight container in the refrigerator for up to 3 days.

Khao Mok Gai

Chicken Biryani

Serves 4

Khao mok gai is Thailand's version of chicken biryani and is particularly popular among the Muslim population of southern Thailand. Traditionally, this dish begins with raw, toasted rice that's dyed a vivid yellow hue thanks to turmeric and saffron, making it a perfect centerpiece for dinner. The yogurt-marinated chicken is gently poached so it maintains its juiciness when all components are steamed together in one pot. My version is quite efficient because it begins with day-old rice and a sauce that takes five minutes to stir together rather than hours of simmering. Instead of poaching the chicken within the rice, I serve the grilled chicken separately. All the highlights of the classic khao mok gai, but way less fussy.

For the khao mok curry sauce:

- 1 tablespoon Madras curry powder
- ½ teaspoon ground turmeric
- 1 tablespoon Magic Powder (aka Asian chicken bouillon)
- ½ cup (120 ml) warm water

For the rice:

- ¼ cup (40 g) roasted, unsalted peanuts
- 2 tablespoons Garlic Oil (page 65)
- 2 tablespoons chopped white onion
- 1 tablespoon chopped garlic
- 1 tablespoon minced, peeled fresh ginger
- 2 cups (280 g) day-old steamed rice
- ¼ cup (35 g) cooked chickpeas (homemade or canned, drained and rinsed)
- ½ cup (40 g) Fried Shallots (page 64), or store-bought fried shallots, plus more for serving
- 1 teaspoon sugar
- ½ teaspoon kosher salt

For serving:

- Gai Yang (Bangkok BBQ Chicken, page 111)
- 3 scallions, green and white parts, thinly sliced
- Fresh cilantro sprigs
- Fresh mint leaves
- Cucumber Achaar (page 196)

MAKE THE KHAO MOK CURRY SAUCE:

In a medium bowl, combine the curry powder, turmeric, magic powder, and warm water and stir until the spices are dissolved. Set aside.

MAKE THE RICE:

In a medium bowl, soak the peanuts in ½ cup (120 ml) water for 30 minutes or up to overnight.

In a large skillet, heat the garlic oil over medium heat. Add the onion, garlic, and ginger and cook, stirring, until softened and fragrant, about 1 minute. Drain the soaked peanuts and add them to the pan along with the cooked rice. Toss to combine and cook until heated through, about another 2 minutes. Gently fold in the chickpeas and khao mok curry sauce, stirring, until the rice turns yellow (you may not need all the sauce—it depends on how dry your rice is). Add the fried shallots, sugar, and salt and continue to toss the rice until evenly combined.

TO SERVE:

Place the rice on an oval serving platter. Top with the gai yang and garnish with scallions, cilantro, mint, and fried shallots and serve with cucumber achaar. Store any leftover chicken in an airtight container in the refrigerator for up to 4 days.

Pad Gratiem Prik Thai

Garlic Pepper Stir-Fry

Serves 2 to 4

Whenever I'm busy—with the baby, the restaurant, or writing—this is what I make. It's the most simple, basic thing and requires very little of my pantry and fridge. In fact, this is my go-to when I haven't been grocery shopping in a while. Although this dish requires minimal ingredients and minimal work, it still perfectly satiates my cravings for punchy, garlicky Thai food. When I'm on the go, I love to pack this dish away in my stainless-steel tiffin, a traditional and stackable Thai lunch box. This will be a favorite weeknight dinner or quick lunch for you, too.

2 tablespoons neutral oil, such as sunflower

4 cloves garlic, smashed and peeled

½ cup (60 g) chopped white onion

8 ounces (225 g) skinless, boneless chicken thighs, chopped into bite-sized pieces

1 tablespoon sugar

1 tablespoon oyster sauce

1 tablespoon Thai seasoning sauce

¼ teaspoon ground white pepper

For serving:

1 tablespoon Fried Garlic (page 65), or store-bought fried garlic

Chopped fresh cilantro

Cucumber slices

Steamed rice (see page 36)

In a large skillet, heat the oil and garlic over high heat until the garlic starts to turn golden, about 4 minutes. Add the onion and cook until it is slightly opaque, about another 2 minutes. Add the chicken, and when the chicken begins to turn white, about 2 minutes, add the sugar, oyster sauce, Thai seasoning sauce, and white pepper and continue cooking until the chicken is cooked through and well coated in the sauce, about 3 minutes.

TO SERVE:

Transfer to a serving platter and garnish with fried garlic, cilantro, and cucumber slices on the side. Serve with steamed rice. Leftovers will keep in an airtight container in the refrigerator for up to 4 days.

Bacon Pad Krapao

Spicy Bacon Basil Stir-Fry

Serves 4

When Thais don't know what they're in the mood to eat, they order pad krapao. An undisputed favorite in Thailand for everyone—college students, parents who need to fix something quick for dinner, streetside vendors—it takes less than fifteen minutes to come together, and the result is what all good Thai food should be: fragrant, punchy, and as spicy as you want it to be. The fun thing about krapao is that you can use any kind of protein. Minced pork and chicken are traditional, but as a true Southern man, I've adapted this recipe to use locally sourced bacon. The bacon I get from Tennessee farms is divine against fresh Thai basil, the heat of Thai chiles, and the garlicky sauce that coats each piece of pork. Crown this dish with a runny fried egg like the queen that she is.

For the krapao sauce:

- 2 tablespoons oyster sauce
- 2 tablespoons black soy sauce
- 2 tablespoons fish sauce

For the bacon pad krapao:

- 4 ounces (340 g / about 3 slices) thick-cut bacon, cut into 1-inch (2.5 cm) pieces
- 8 ounces (225 g) ground pork
- 2 tablespoons chopped white onion
- 1 tablespoon finely chopped garlic
- 2 to 3 fresh red Thai chiles, chopped
- 4 ounces (115 g) green beans, ends trimmed and cut into ½-inch (12 mm) pieces (about ¾ cup)
- ½ cup (65 g) coarsely chopped red bell pepper
- ½ cup (65 g) coarsely chopped green bell pepper
- ¼ cup (8 g) fresh Thai basil leaves, torn in half
- 1 teaspoon sugar
- ½ teaspoon ground white pepper

For serving:

- Steamed rice (see page 36)
- 4 fried eggs

MAKE THE KRAPAO SAUCE:

In a small bowl, combine the oyster sauce, black soy sauce, and fish sauce and whisk until combined.

MAKE THE BACON PAD KRAPAO:

In a large skillet, cook the bacon over medium heat, stirring occasionally, until it is partially cooked, 2 to 3 minutes. Using a slotted spoon, transfer the bacon to a paper towel–lined plate or wire rack.

Increase the heat to high and add the ground pork and onion to the pan. Cook, stirring occasionally, until the pork is two-thirds cooked and the onion is translucent, about 2 minutes. Add the garlic and chiles and cook until fragrant, about 30 seconds. Add the reserved bacon, the green beans, red and green peppers, Thai basil, krapao sauce, sugar, and white pepper and cook until the peppers are softened and everything is well combined, about another 1 minute.

TO SERVE:

Transfer to a platter and serve with steamed rice and fried eggs. Store leftovers in an airtight container in the refrigerator for up to 4 days.

FROM TOP:
Bacon Pad Krapao (opposite),
Koong Pad Prik Pao (page 134)

Koong Pad Prik Pao
Roasted Chile Jam Stir-Fry with Shrimp

Serves 4

Nam prik pao is a roasted chile jam that has incredible smoky flavor and subtle sweetness that makes it one of my favorite flavor starters to toss in a wok. You can find it in most Asian grocery stores. It's not quite as aggressive as a red curry paste, nor is the heat as fiery as a standard pad krapao because the chiles are cooked down rather than fresh. When it hits the wok, the jam melts into a sticky glaze that is perfect for coating any protein. In this recipe, I pair it with shrimp, which is an ideal subtly sweet vehicle to deliver pad prik pao to your mouth.

- 2 tablespoons neutral oil, such as sunflower
- 8 ounces (225 g) large (21/25) shrimp, shelled and deveined
- ¼ cup (30 g) sliced white onion
- 1 tablespoon chopped garlic
- 4 dried whole Thai chiles
- 3 fresh makrut lime leaves, ribs removed, torn
- 2 tablespoons nam prik pao (roasted chile jam)
- 4 ounces (115 g) green beans, ends trimmed and cut into 1-inch (2.5 cm) pieces (about ¾ cup)
- 1 cup (115 g) sliced red and green bell pepper
- 1½ teaspoons oyster sauce
- ½ teaspoon sugar
- 12 fresh Thai basil leaves

In a large skillet, heat the oil over high heat until it shimmers. Add the shrimp and onion and cook, stirring occasionally, until the shrimp turns opaque and is slightly seared (you should see it beginning to brown), about 2 minutes. Add the garlic, Thai chiles, lime leaves, nam prik pao, and 2 tablespoons water and cook until the sauce becomes thick and jammy, about 2 minutes. Add the green beans, red and green peppers, oyster sauce, and sugar and toss everything together for 1 minute, or until fully incorporated. Fold in the Thai basil and serve immediately.

Pad See Eiw
Soy Sauce Noodles

Serves 4

As more people have become hip to Thai food, they've begun abandoning the classics that got them hooked on the cuisine in the first place. I'm all for skipping pad Thai, but pad see eiw is a kid favorite that I will never give up on. The char on the chewy rice noodles, the fresh and leafy gai lan, and the fluffy bites of egg make this dish a textural masterpiece. I've never gotten sick of it. *Pad* means stir-fry or wok-fry, and *see ew* means soy sauce, so the dish is exactly what it claims to be. One thing I love about it is that it goes with pretty much every protein: chicken works great, fatty cuts of pork, beef, shrimp, tofu—everything goes here. I even occasionally swap the rice noodles for pappardelle, for a Thai-Talian twist I've coined as "papp see eiw." In fact, you can really use any size rice noodle (although wide, flat noodles are most traditional). Although pad see eiw is hard to make at home without really high heat and a wok, it's still possible to replicate it and get the street vendor vibes you want by using a stainless-steel skillet that can heat evenly and stay hot throughout the cooking process. In true Thai fashion, this dish gets finished with prik nam som (chile vinegar).

For the noodles:

1 (8-ounce / 225 g) package dried long, flat rice noodles (or use fresh noodles or dried pappardelle; see headnote)

For the oyster–soy sauce chicken:

½ cup (120 ml) oyster sauce

¼ cup (60 ml) Thai seasoning sauce or lite soy sauce

¼ cup (60 ml) black soy sauce

2 tablespoons sugar

6 ounces (170 g) skinless, boneless chicken thighs, sliced (about 2 thighs)

For the stir-fry:

2 tablespoons neutral oil, such as sunflower

2 large eggs

4 ounces (115 g) firm or extra-firm tofu, drained and cut into ¼-inch (6 mm) wide rectangles

¼ white onion, sliced

2 tablespoons finely chopped garlic

2 cups (115 g) mixed mushrooms, such as trumpet, oyster, shiitake, and cremini, trimmed and sliced

3½ cups (4 ounces / 115 g) gai lan (Chinese broccoli), cut into 2-inch (5 cm) pieces

4 scallions, pale green and white parts, cut into 1-inch (2.5 cm) pieces

½ teaspoon ground white pepper

For serving:

Fried Garlic (page 65), or store-bought fried garlic

Ground white pepper

Prik Nam Som (Chile Vinegar, page 54)

(Recipe continues)

MAKE THE NOODLES:

Put the noodles in a large bowl and pour warm water over them. Let stand until soft, 20 to 30 minutes. Drain and set aside. Just before cooking, fill a large saucepan three-quarters full of water and bring to a boil over high heat.

MAKE THE OYSTER–SOY SAUCE CHICKEN:

In a medium, nonreactive bowl, combine the oyster sauce, Thai seasoning sauce, black soy sauce, and sugar and stir until the sugar is dissolved. Coat the chicken with ¼ cup (60 ml) of the sauce and let stand for 5 minutes to marinate. Reserve the remaining sauce.

STIR-FRY THE NOODLES:

In a large skillet, heat the oil over high heat until it shimmers. Crack the eggs into the pan and cook until the whites begin to set and the yolks harden, breaking them slightly (they're not scrambled in pieces but more like a broken omelet). Add the marinated chicken and cook, stirring occasionally, until the chicken is opaque, about 2 minutes. Add the tofu, onion, and garlic and continue cooking, stirring frequently, until fragrant, about 30 seconds. Add the mushrooms, gai lan, and scallions and stir until combined. Stir in the white pepper.

Blanch the drained rice noodles in the boiling water for 10 to 15 seconds (see Note for fresh noodles). Drain the noodles, transfer them to the skillet, and stir together. Drizzle in as much of the remaining oyster–soy sauce as desired, adjust to taste (keeping in mind that the sauce will reduce and intensify as it heats), and cook until the sauce deepens in color and the noodles are tender, about 2 minutes. Stir to combine.

TO SERVE:

Transfer to a platter and then garnish with fried garlic and white pepper, and serve immediately with a side of prik nam som.

Note: If using fresh noodles, place them directly into the skillet—there is no need to soak them or blanch them in boiling water. Or to make "papp" see eiw, cook pappardelle noodles according to the package instructions and place them directly into the skillet when the noodles are added.

Pad Kee Mao
Drunken Spaghetti

Serves 4

There are a couple theories about why drunken noodles earned their name. One is that spicy food is what you crave while drinking (this checks out—Thai people love spicy foods any time of day, but especially when they're drunk). Another is that they are the perfect hangover cure. Whatever the reason, you don't need a night out to enjoy this dish. To make it my own, I use an Italian ingredient, spaghetti, instead of the traditional rice noodles—Thai-talian fusion at its best. Spaghetti is actually a common variation in modern Thai cooking. It is so easy to work with and absorbs the garlicky, spicy notes of pad kee mao well. If you really want to lean into the fusion identity of this dish, pair it with a negroni or spritz!

1 tablespoon neutral oil, such as sunflower

6 ounces (170 g) large (21/25) shrimp, shelled and deveined

¼ white onion, sliced

4 ounces (115 g) gai lan (Chinese broccoli), stems and leaves, cut into 2-inch (5 cm) pieces (about 2 cups)

1 tablespoon chopped garlic

½ teaspoon chopped fresh Thai chile (about 1 chile)

8 ounces (225 g) spaghetti, cooked according to package instructions

1 Roma tomato (about 5½ ounces / 155 g), cut into 8 wedges

1 cup (20 g) fresh Thai basil leaves

¼ cup (60 ml) oyster sauce

¼ cup (60 ml) black soy sauce

1 tablespoon fish sauce

1 teaspoon sugar

⅛ teaspoon ground white pepper

Fried Garlic (page 65), or store-bought fried garlic

In a large skillet, heat the oil over high heat until it shimmers. Add the shrimp and onion and cook, stirring, until the shrimp turns opaque and begins to brown, about 2 minutes. Add the gai lan, garlic, and Thai chile and cook, stirring, for 1 minute, or until the garlic is fragrant, being careful not to let the garlic burn. Add the spaghetti, tomato, Thai basil, oyster sauce, soy sauce, fish sauce, sugar, and white pepper and toss continuously until the tomatoes begin to break down and the Thai basil begins to wilt, about 2 minutes. If needed, add a splash of water to loosen everything up. Once the spaghetti is hot, transfer to a serving platter, garnish with fried garlic, and serve immediately.

Mom's Pad Macaroni

Serves 4 to 6

My mom used to make this dish whenever I had friends over as a kid. It used to mortify me—why couldn't we order pizza instead?—but my friends loved it, and I've grown to love it, too. This is a recipe that truly highlights how adaptive Thai immigrants are and is a jewel among the Thai American diaspora. Penne, ziti, and rigatoni work great as well. The pasta gets coated in a glossy ketchup and sriracha sauce, and pops of sweetness can be found in the stir-fried onions, tomatoes, and carrots. I like to think of it as red sauce meets pad Thai.

For the sauce:

¼ cup (60 ml) ketchup

2 tablespoons Sriracha (page 60), or store-bought sriracha

2 tablespoons Thai seasoning sauce

1 teaspoon sugar

½ teaspoon ground white pepper

For the macaroni:

2 tablespoons neutral oil, such as sunflower

2 large eggs

8 ounces (225 g) sliced chicken thighs (or protein of your choice)

¼ white onion, sliced

1 medium carrot, peeled and thinly sliced on the bias

1 tablespoon finely chopped garlic

1 Roma tomato (about 5½ ounces / 155 g), cut into wedges

2 cups (225 g) cooked pasta, such as macaroni, penne, or ziti

2 scallions, green and white parts, cut into 1-inch (2.5 cm) pieces

MAKE THE SAUCE:

In a medium bowl, combine the ketchup, sriracha, Thai seasoning sauce, sugar, and white pepper. Set aside.

MAKE THE MACARONI:

In a large skillet, heat the oil over high heat. Gently crack in the eggs and lightly scramble until just set, about 1 minute. Transfer to a plate and set aside.

Add the chicken, onion, and carrot to the pan and cook until the chicken is halfway cooked, about 2 minutes. Push everything to one side of the pan, then add the garlic and cook, stirring, for 30 seconds. Add the tomato, pasta, and scallions and return the scrambled eggs to the pan. Pour the sauce over the mixture and cook, stirring occasionally, until the chicken is cooked through and everything is well coated, about 2 minutes. Serve immediately. Store leftovers in an airtight container in the refrigerator for up to 3 days.

SODA
SINGHA
SODA

Pad Brussels Sprouts Fai Dang
Wok-fired Greens with Chiles

Serves 2 to 4

One of the best vegetable side dishes in Thai cooking is pad pak boong fai dang, or stir-fried morning glory with a soybean glaze and streaks of Thai chiles. Because it's not always easy to source this leafy green, also known as water spinach, I love recreating this dish with a vegetable that we love in the South, Brussels sprouts. Brussels sprouts are sturdy enough to withstand the heat of the wok and the layers of leaves can really absorb the fermented bean paste. You can also use heartier greens like Swiss chard, Tuscan kale, or collard greens. Adjust the chiles to your heat preference, and make sure to finish with a sprinkling of fried shallots. Also, remember this dish is *fast*. Once the onions are sweated down, everything comes together in minutes, so make sure you have your mise en place for this one.

For the sauce:

- 2 tablespoons thao jiew (fermented soybean paste)
- 2 tablespoons Pickled Garlic (page 62)
- 1 tablespoon Thai seasoning sauce
- 1 tablespoon sugar

For the Brussels sprouts:

- 2 tablespoons neutral oil, such as sunflower
- ¼ white onion, sliced
- 8 ounces (225 g) Brussels sprouts, trimmed and cut in half (quarter larger ones)
- 1 tablespoon finely chopped garlic
- 3 fresh red Thai chiles, split in half
- 2 tablespoons Fried Shallots (page 64), or store-bought fried shallots, plus more for serving

MAKE THE SAUCE:

In a small bowl, combine the thao jiew, pickled garlic, seasoning sauce, and sugar. Set aside.

MAKE THE BRUSSELS SPROUTS:

In a large skillet, heat the oil over high heat. Add the onion and Brussels sprouts and cook, stirring once or twice but not often, as you want the Brussels sprouts to char while the onion softens, about 4 minutes. Add the garlic and Thai chiles and stir to combine. Once fragrant, add the sauce and fried shallots and quickly toss to combine. Stir in 2 tablespoons water to loosen the sauce and cook for 1 minute more. Remove from the heat, garnish with fried shallots, and serve immediately. Store leftovers in an airtight container in the refrigerator for up to 4 days.

Pad Sataw

Stink Bean and Asparagus Stir-Fry

Serves 4

This is a dish that makes its presence known and tends to linger. Stink bean, or *sataw* in Thai, very much lives up to its name. Its pungent odor and bitter flavor remind me, in some ways, of durian or stinky tofu: The smell might be offensive to some, but the flavor is complex and fascinating to others. And to up the challenge, you'll find a dollop of shrimp paste in this recipe, too. Since we're starting off with such a strong aroma, I thought I'd make this dish more approachable by adding a universally beloved mellow vegetable, asparagus. The asparagus tones down the immediate funk of the stink bean. This dish will push your palate and cling to you the morning after, but perhaps you'll fall in love with that clinginess a little.

1 tablespoon neutral oil, such as sunflower

¼ cup (30 g) sliced white onion

6 ounces (170 g) large shrimp, shelled and deveined (about ½ cup)

4 ounces (115 g) ground pork

1 tablespoon chopped garlic

1 teaspoon chopped fresh Thai chile

1 teaspoon shrimp paste

6 makrut lime leaves: 3 whole leaves hand-ripped to the spine and 3 ribs removed and thinly sliced

1 cup (77 g) sa-tor (stink beans)

4 spears asparagus, trimmed and cut on the bias into 2-inch (5 cm) pieces

1 tablespoon fish sauce

1 teaspoon Magic Powder (aka Asian chicken bouillon)

1 tablespoon sugar

2 Fresno chiles, thinly sliced

Steamed rice (see page 36), for serving

In a large skillet, heat the oil over high heat. Add the onion and shrimp and cook, stirring occasionally, until the shrimp turns opaque and is slightly seared (you should see it beginning to brown), about 2 minutes. Add the pork, garlic, Thai chile, shrimp paste, whole makrut lime leaves, and 2 tablespoons water and cook, stirring, until the pork is cooked through, about 3 minutes. Add the sa-tor, asparagus, fish sauce, magic powder, and sugar and cook, stirring everything together, until the vegetables are just tender, about 1 minute. Stir in the Fresno chiles and cook, stirring, until everything is well combined, another minute. Garnish with the thinly sliced makrut lime leaves and serve immediately with steamed rice. Store leftovers in an airtight container in the refrigerator for up to 4 days.

My International Market story:

By Cate Thompson

Back in the late 70s, my grandparents were cleaning out my great-grandfather's home (now the current international market location). Belly a-grumblin', my grandpa, John Garnam, walked across the street to scope out the international market buffet. Then, a family staple came to be. My grandpa & Patti became great friends. He took cooking classes from her and learned to make those dynamite eggrolls which he later taught me to make. We used to go to IM on Christmas Eve and most Sundays. It was and is a special part of Nashville for our family. I am thrilled for this reopening and can't wait to continue the legacy.

♡ ♡ ♡♡ ♡

Southern Traditions

International Market sold its original location to Belmont University after decades of the school building their campus around our family's business. Shortly after the sale, my mother passed away. It was a bittersweet moment, and the outpouring of sympathy from the community was both incredibly beautiful and overwhelming at the same time.

When my sister, Anna, and I decided to continue the business (with me in the kitchen and her tackling front-of-house operations), we did not anticipate the number of stories our customers would share about mom on a daily basis. It seemed like everyone had a memory to share about her and the restaurant itself. Although the sentiment came from a place of celebration and nostalgia, my sister and I were in a grieving process after losing our mother and, admittedly, it was emotionally draining.

One day, Anna mentioned that her therapist suggested putting out comment cards for the guests, encouraging them to document their fondest International Market memory. This way, customers could still share their stories without unloading a heavy, emotional burden on us two kids who were missing our mom and still trying to run a restaurant through all of it.

The response resulted in a massive collection of the most precious, heartfelt memories that truly celebrate the breadth and impact International Market has had. It made me realize that though a restaurant is primarily a place that serves food, in certain instances, what stems beyond the food is where a lasting impression is made. Here are some of my favorite memories from those comment cards.

Yes, Chef!
International Market
and Restaurant
nashville, Tennessee
since 1975
International Market
and Restaurant
nashville, Tennessee
since 1975

FROM "JOE"

International Market has been a mainstay for me and a reliable, steady presence in my life. My parents got divorced when I was young, and Dad moved to Green Hills. Weekends with him meant Sportsman's on Friday and International Market on Sundays. Broccoli noodle, pepper steak, and egg roll.

When I went to college, I stayed close and went to Vanderbilt. My very first apartment was on Belmont—dangerously close to International Market. Broccoli noodle, hot cabbage with pork, and tofu curry. Far too often.

After college, I got my first job and moved to Bellevue. But I still made the trek on a semi-regular basis (if not as often as before). Broccoli noodle, hot cabbage with pork, shu mai with all the toppings (that garlic!).

Once I got married, I moved back to the neighborhood with my new wife, who grew up two blocks down from Belmont. She was a regular, too. We would stop by after yard sales on Saturday, always sneaking in a little early at 10:30 or 10:45. No one minded, and they always served us anyway. Broccoli noodle, hot cabbage with pork, pad woon cent, vegetable curry roll.

Then we had a kid. Our days of going out were on hold, so we developed a nasty takeout habit. Every Friday was International Market, and after many long years of eating from the line, I finally graduated to the menu. Pad Thai with pork, extra spicy, and a vegetable curry roll.

Just writing all this out, I can't believe how long I've been eating your mom's food and how important it has been to my life.

FROM VIVIAN WHITE:

I moved away from Nashville twenty-five years ago, but I will credit the International Market for getting me out. Here's how:

My mom was raising two of us on her own. She worked long hours for minimum wage and was often not home in the evenings. Early on, she told us our grades were our responsibility, especially getting our homework done every night without being asked.

The only reason we did our homework each night was for the chance to get our report cards back every six weeks. If we got all As and Bs, we could go out that very night to the International Market. It was her way of treating us for the work we were all putting in. Oh, the tears of missing the dinner if we got a C! It only happened a few times because we cared so much about this treat.

You all kept the prices low, gave us such generous portions, and made it possible for her to take us out to a "fancy dinner." Now I see she saved for weeks and probably skipped a lot of things for herself for that special occasion every month and a half. Once she didn't have enough and stopped by a friend's house to borrow the cash—something she never did in her life, but she knew the importance of this ritual.

So, along with my indomitable mom, I credit the International Market for teaching me to be a good student. It worked—I'm now an astrophysicist! Thank you all so much for making our lives sparkle six times each year.

My mom is the heart and soul of International Market. In 1975, despite the lack of a blueprint or a surrounding Thai community, she had the vision of bringing a Thai restaurant to life for Nashville. She was a pioneer, a woman who truly changed the face of Nashville's dining scene. Her cafeteria was a legendary introduction to Thai flavors and street food culture; some of her menu items are still crowd-pleasers at International Market today.

Thais commonly have quick lunches or early dinners at a raan khao gaeng, or a rice-curry shop, choosing between two or three different curries, stir-fries, and noodles presented in steel bins and served with a side of steamed jasmine rice. I think of a khao gaeng shop as the equivalent of a "meat and three" cafeteria in the American South, where comfort foods like meatloaf and fried chicken are paired with macaroni and cheese, green beans, and hush puppies. At both, diners get a deal and a fast meal they've customized to their tastes. In this chapter, you'll find my mom's classic khao gaeng dishes; I've also added some of my own twists that are intended to be eaten with rice. And yes, there are even a couple noodle dishes. If you've been coming to International Market since its inception, a lot of these recipes might seem familiar, and even nostalgic. The best part about these recipes is how easy they are to prepare. Before you start tackling these dishes, just like in the wok chapter (pages 122 to 144), it is important that your mise en place is ready to go. And be sure to read over the recipe a few times before you start cooking, since these recipes come together quite quickly.

Mom's Broccoli Noodle

Serves 4

If there's something Patti was good at, it was giving the people what they wanted. My mom knew that as she introduced Thai food to Nashville there might be hesitation from folks who had never heard of, seen, or tried Thai food. These broccoli noodles were her solution because the beef and broccoli combination had already been introduced through Chinese American cuisine. I see this as a simplified version of pad see eiw, and it fared well in the steam table at International Market's earliest iteration. Back then Patti incorporated beef, but on the current lunch line, I omitted the protein to offer a delicious vegetarian option (be sure to opt for seasoning sauce instead of fish sauce to make this dish truly vegetarian).

8 ounces (225 g) flat, wide rice noodles

½ cup (120 ml) neutral oil, such as sunflower

1 tablespoon finely chopped garlic

1 pound (455 g) sirloin steak, trimmed, thinly sliced, and cut into 1-inch (2.5 cm) strips

1 pound (455 g) broccoli, cut into 1-inch (2.5 cm) florets

2 tablespoons sweet soy sauce

1 tablespoon black soy sauce

2 tablespoons fish sauce or Thai seasoning sauce

2 tablespoons sugar

1 teaspoon kosher salt

Put the rice noodles in a large bowl and cover them with warm water. Let stand until soft, 20 to 30 minutes. Drain and set aside.

Bring a medium saucepan filled three-quarters with water to a boil over high heat.

In a large skillet, heat the oil over high heat. Add the garlic and cook, stirring, until fragrant, being careful not to let it burn, about 30 seconds. Add the steak and cook until halfway cooked, 1 to 2 minutes.

Meanwhile, add the broccoli to the boiling water and cook for 1 to 2 minutes to blanch it. Using a spider or slotted spoon, remove it and transfer to the skillet with the steak. Stir to combine.

Add the rice noodles to the same boiling water and cook for 10 to 15 seconds. Using a spider or slotted spoon, remove it, add to the skillet, and stir to combine.

Lower the heat to medium. Add the sweet soy sauce, black soy sauce, fish sauce, sugar, and salt and cook, stirring, until fully combined, about 2 minutes. Serve immediately.

Mom's Pepper Steak

Serves 4 to 6

This pepper steak, which is more like an Asian take on a Southern beef stew, remains on the steam table to this day. I don't quite know how to define this dish—it has Thai influences, sure, but also some parts of it are Chinese American coded, while others feel truly Southern. Whatever the case, this has been a staple of International Market for decades. There's one customer who has been coming in since he was a kid—and he is now well into adulthood—and he only orders this dish. This recipe is a nod to him.

2 tablespoons cornstarch

½ cup (120 ml) neutral oil, such as sunflower

1 pound (455 g) sirloin steak, trimmed, thinly sliced, and cut into 1-inch (2.5 cm) strips

1 cup (124 g) coarsely chopped white onion

1 cup (115 g) thinly sliced carrots

4 cloves garlic, finely chopped

2 cups (250 g) coarsely chopped red and green bell pepper

2 tablespoons black soy sauce

3 tablespoons oyster sauce

1 tablespoon sugar

1 teaspoon Magic Powder (aka Asian chicken bouillon)

1 teaspoon ground black pepper

½ cup (120 ml) Nam Sai (Clear Bone Broth, page 178) or water, plus more if needed

Steamed rice (see page 36)

First, make a cornstarch slurry: Put the cornstarch in a small bowl, add 2 tablespoons water, and whisk to dissolve. Set aside.

In a large skillet, heat the oil over high heat. Once the oil is hot, add the sliced steak and cook, turning once, to brown both sides, about 2 minutes. Add the onions, carrots, and garlic and cook until fragrant, about 2 minutes. Add the red and green pepper, black soy sauce, oyster sauce, sugar, magic powder, and black pepper and toss to evenly combine. Add the nam sai and bring to a simmer. Slowly drizzle in the cornstarch slurry and cook, stirring, until it thickens like a gravy, about 1 minute. (Add more nam sai to loosen the sauce if it's too thick.)

Transfer to a large platter and serve immediately with steamed rice. Store leftovers in an airtight container in the refrigerator for up to 3 days.

Mom's Broccoli Chicken

Serves 4 to 6

It's broccoli, it's chicken, it's water chestnuts, and it's a little zany brilliance. What's not to like? When my mom first came to Nashville, she lived with an American family with a very food-savvy grandma. It was there that she was exposed to classic Southern fare, from pies to casseroles, for the first time. With practice, my mom was able to mimic those casseroles—but with Asian flavors—for her customers. The closest thing I can compare this recipe to is a broccoli cheddar casserole, but with oyster sauce and fish sauce instead of cheese. It's creamy, loaded with chicken and broccoli, and has plenty of umami.

- 2 tablespoons cornstarch
- ¼ cup (60 ml) neutral oil, such as sunflower
- 1 cup (110 g) sliced white onion
- 2 medium skinless, boneless chicken breast halves (1 pound / 455 g), thinly sliced
- 6 cloves garlic, chopped
- 6 cups (335 g) broccoli florets
- 1 (8-ounce / 225 g) can sliced water chestnuts, drained
- 2 tablespoons oyster sauce
- 2 tablespoons thao jiew (fermented soybean paste)
- 1 tablespoon Thai seasoning sauce
- 1 tablespoon sugar
- ½ teaspoon ground white pepper
- ½ cup (120 ml) Nam Sai (Clear Bone Broth, page 178) or water, plus more if needed
- Steamed rice (see page 36), for serving

Bring a medium saucepan filled three-quarters with water to a boil over high heat.

Make a cornstarch slurry: Put the cornstarch in a small bowl, add 2 tablespoons water, and whisk to dissolve. Set aside.

In a large skillet, heat the oil over high heat until it shimmers. Add the onions and cook until translucent, about 2 minutes. Add the chicken and cook, stirring occasionally, until the slices begin to brown on all sides, about 2 minutes. Add the garlic and cook for an additional 2 minutes.

Meanwhile, add the broccoli to the boiling water and cook for 1 to 2 minutes to blanch. Using a spider or slotted spoon, transfer to the skillet with the chicken and stir to combine.

Add the water chestnuts, oyster sauce, thao jiew, Thai seasoning sauce, sugar, and white pepper and stir well to combine. Pour in the nam sai (or water) and bring to a simmer. Cook until the flavors combine and the chicken is cooked through, about 4 minutes.

Finish the dish by slowly drizzling in the cornstarch slurry, whisking it in a teaspoon at a time, just until the sauce thickens, about 1 minute. Add more broth (or water) to loosen the sauce if it's too thick. Serve immediately with steamed rice. Store leftovers in an airtight container in the refrigerator for up to 3 days.

Mom's Bamboo Chicken

Serves 4 to 6

This chicken curry dish is a celebration of aromatics. Although coconut milk is great for many curry applications, you won't find any here—the curry paste is the star without any dilution. The reason I don't typically carry this dish in the restaurant now (despite getting requests from customers) is that it is comprised primarily of processed, canned products. However, this is the perfect easy recipe for a beginner home cook to attempt; it's extremely approachable and the resulting dish has explosive flavors.

1 (16-ounce / 455 g) package bamboo shoot tips, prepared per the instructions on page 18

¼ cup (60 ml) neutral oil, such as sunflower

¼ cup (65 g) red curry paste

2 medium skinless, boneless chicken breast halves (1 pound / 455 g), thinly sliced

½ medium white onion, sliced

2 tablespoons fish sauce

1 teaspoon sugar

½ teaspoon Magic Powder (aka Asian chicken bouillon)

4 fresh makrut lime leaves, ribs removed and thinly sliced

1 cup (240 ml) Nam Sai (Clear Bone Broth, page 178) or water (optional)

Steamed rice (see page 36), for serving

Using two forks, shred the prepared bamboo shoots into smaller strips, like pulled pork.

Heat the oil in a large skillet over medium heat until it shimmers. Add the red curry paste and stir until it becomes fragrant and the color deepens, about 1 minute. Add the chicken and cook, stirring occasionally, until halfway cooked, about 2 minutes. Stir in the onion, shredded bamboo shoots, fish sauce, sugar, magic powder, and lime leaves and continue to cook until the chicken is cooked through, about 3 minutes. Add the nam sai, if you want the dish saucy, and simmer for an additional 3 minutes to marry the flavors.

Serve immediately, with steamed rice. Store leftovers in an airtight container in the refrigerator for up to 3 days.

Kai Jeaow
Thai Omelet

Makes 1 (8-inch / 20 cm) omelet; serves 2

If you're searching for a recipe with the best ratio of ease of preparation to delicious payoff, you've found it. The Thai omelet is a kid-friendly classic, a midnight meal, and a welcome side dish all in one. Yes, you can eat this at breakfast, but it's also the perfect accompaniment to a midnight bowl of jhok (page 186) or a fiery plate of stir-fried morning glory (see page 142 for my take on this dish). In almost every family sit-down meal in Thailand, you'll find kai jeaow. The key here is hot oil, which sounds scary but is pretty easy as long as you're careful. You want to lower the beaten eggs gently into the hot oil, which causes the eggs to puff up. You are looking for crunchy edges and a fluffy center. The fun part about this recipe is that it's incredible as written, but you can also add ground pork with white pepper, crab meat, and/or Thai chiles.

- 3 large eggs
- 1 teaspoon fish sauce
- ½ teaspoon sugar
- ½ teaspoon Magic Powder (aka Asian chicken bouillon)
- Pinch of ground white pepper
- 2 tablespoons neutral oil, such as sunflower
- ¼ cup (55 g) chopped shrimp
- 8 slices white onion
- 1 tablespoon chopped preserved sweet radish
- 4 slices Roma tomato
- 1 scallion, white and green parts, thinly sliced

For serving:

- Fried Garlic (page 65), or store-bought fried garlic
- Fresh cilantro sprigs
- Cucumber slices
- Lime cheeks (see page 50)
- Sriracha (page 60), or store-bought sriracha
- Prik Nam Pla (Chile Fish Sauce, page 56)
- Steamed rice (see page 36)

Preheat the oven to 350°F (175°C).

In a large bowl, beat the eggs, fish sauce, sugar, magic powder, and white pepper with a wire whisk.

In an oven-safe nonstick 8-inch (20 cm) skillet, heat the 1 tablespoon oil over medium heat until it shimmers. Add the shrimp and cook, stirring occasionally, until the shrimp begins to turn opaque, about 1 minute. Remove and set aside. To the same skillet, add 1 tablespoon oil. Add the onion and cook until translucent, about 2 minutes. Gently pour in the omelet batter. As the egg begins to set, use the spatula to pull the edges of the omelet toward the center and let the eggs run underneath. Sprinkle in the sweet radish and continue pulling until the bottom of the eggs are set but the surface is still runny, about 2 minutes. Evenly place the tomatoes, the scallions, and the reserved shrimp in the omelet and cook until eggs are no longer runny and the edges begin to release from the skillet, another 1 to 2 minutes.

Transfer the skillet to the oven and cook until deep brown and crispy, about 5 minutes.

TO SERVE:

Transfer to a serving plate and garnish with the fried garlic. Serve with cilantro, cucumber slices, lime cheeks, sriracha, prik nam pla, and steamed rice on the side.

Mom's Tofu Cabbage

Serves 4 to 6

In the South, braised cabbage is commonly found in restaurants and at home. This is why I think this dish resonates with so many of our customers. It's a go-to and a nostalgic one. This recipe is really simple, delicious, and comforting. At its core, it's feel-good Southern food with a Thai twist. Although my mom traditionally made it with pork shoulder, I like to swap the pork with tofu. This dish tastes its best on day two or three, after the cabbage has plenty of time to absorb all the flavors.

¼ cup (60 ml) neutral oil, such as sunflower

2 tablespoons red curry paste

1 cup (240 ml) vegetable stock or water

4 cups (410 g) chopped green cabbage

2 tablespoons Thai seasoning sauce

1 tablespoon sugar

½ teaspoon kosher salt

½ teaspoon Magic Powder (aka Asian chicken bouillon)

1 (16-ounce / 455 g) package firm or silken tofu, drained and cut into 1-inch (2.5 cm) cubes

Thinly sliced scallions, green parts, for serving

Steamed rice (see page 36), for serving

Heat the oil in a large skillet with a lid over medium heat. Add the red curry paste and cook, stirring, until fragrant, about 1 minute. Add the stock and stir until the liquid is evenly combined. Add the cabbage, Thai seasoning sauce, sugar, salt, and magic powder and stir to combine. Reduce the heat, cover, and simmer, stirring occasionally, until the cabbage cooks down, at least 10 minutes.

Gently place the tofu into the skillet and, using a large spoon, baste with the red curry sauce until warmed through, 1 to 2 minutes.

Garnish with scallions and serve with steamed rice. Store leftovers in an airtight container in the refrigerator for up to 3 days.

Mom's Eggplant Curry

Serves 4 to 6

Like a good bottle of merlot and a wheel of Parmigiano-Reggiano, this dish gets better with time. Yes, it already tastes great on day one (and you won't be able to resist having a bite because it's so savory). But on day four, this tastes *amazing*—the eggplant breaks down and mingles with the beef and becomes what I can only describe as a red curry version of baba ghanoush meets beef stew. It's simple, easy, and feels like you're eating at a Thai restaurant in Marrakesh. My mom used Italian eggplant for this dish as it was the easiest varietal for her to find, and to this day I've stayed true to her rendition at the restaurant. I love how it continues to break down over time almost to mush. However, at home, I've adapted to include a second textural dimension with firm Thai eggplant. This is a cool recipe for eggplant lovers, and honestly, any variety you find at the market will work.

Kosher salt

6 cups (480 g) cubed Italian or Japanese eggplant (1-inch / 2.5 cm cubes)

¼ cup (60 ml) neutral oil, such as sunflower

2 tablespoons red curry paste

1 pound (455 g) sirloin or chuck steak, trimmed and thinly sliced (optional)

4 Thai eggplants (210 g), quartered (optional)

2 tablespoons oyster sauce

1 teaspoon sugar

½ teaspoon Magic Powder (aka Asian chicken bouillon)

2 jalapeño chiles, thinly sliced

Steamed rice (see page 36), for serving

Bring a medium saucepan filled three-quarters with salted water to a boil over high heat. Add the Italian or Japanese eggplant and cook until reduced in size and starting to turn translucent, 6 to 8 minutes. Drain and transfer to a paper towel–lined baking pan.

Heat the oil in a large skillet over high heat. Add the red curry paste and cook, stirring, until fragrant, about 1 minute. Add the steak and Thai eggplants, if using, the oyster sauce, sugar, and magic powder and cook until the beef is cooked halfway through, about 2 minutes. Reduce the heat to medium. Stir in the boiled eggplant and cook until the eggplant releases its liquid and is tender, 8 to 10 minutes. Just before serving, fold in the jalapeño chiles. Serve immediately with steamed rice. Store leftovers in an airtight container in the refrigerator for up to 3 days.

Mom's Pad Woon Cent

Glass Noodles with Pickled Garlic

Serves 4 to 6

Through all my culinary training, I would never think to pour pickled garlic over noodles and sliced onions and call it a day. It seems like a surefire way to obliterate your palate. But for as long as I can remember, this version of pad woon cent has been a customer favorite. My guess is that my mom wanted to introduce the flavor profile of pad Thai in a way that could withstand a buffet hot bar—so instead of rice noodles, which would harden, she opted for soybean threads (otherwise known as glass noodles). This is not a traditional pad Thai or pad woon cent (otherwise known as stir-fried glass noodles) recipe by any means; this is a Myint invention. The standout flavor here is the pickled garlic, which adds a punchiness that saturates all the thin strands of noodles. Fish sauce and sugar work to balance some of the acid, while chicken and eggs add heft. Although this might be one of the strangest recipes in this whole chapter, let alone in this entire book, when everything comes together, it works. And since it was part of Mom's steam table, it fits under "khao gaeng"—although it doesn't necessarily have to be eaten with rice.

6 ounces (170 g) dry bean thread glass noodles

3 tablespoons neutral oil, such as sunflower

1 cup thinly sliced white onion (about ¼ large onion)

4 cloves garlic, crushed and chopped

1½ cups thinly sliced chicken breast (340 g)

6 large eggs

½ cup (75 g) Pickled Garlic (page 62)

2 tablespoons fish sauce

2 tablespoons sugar

¼ cup (60 ml) vinegar from Pickled Garlic and Vinegar (page 62)

1 teaspoon Magic Powder (aka Asian chicken bouillon)

3 scallions, green and white parts, cut into 1-inch (2.5 cm) pieces

½ teaspoon ground black pepper

Put the bean thread noodles in a large bowl and cover with hot water. Leave until softened, about 20 minutes. Drain, pat dry, and, using kitchen scissors, cut the noodles into 6-inch (15 cm) pieces.

In a large, high-sided sauté pan, heat the oil over medium-high heat. Add the onions, garlic, and chicken and cook, stirring, until the chicken is cooked through, 2 to 3 minutes. Gently crack 3 eggs into the pan and cook, lightly stirring to break the yolks, until the whites are opaque, about 2 minutes. Add the pickled garlic and soaked noodles and toss to combine. Moving the noodles to one side, gently crack the remaining 3 eggs into the pan and lightly scramble, about another 2 minutes.

Stir in the fish sauce, sugar, vinegar, and magic powder. Add the scallions and stir until everything is well combined. Finish with the black pepper and serve immediately. Store any remaining noodles in an airtight container in the refrigerator for up to 1 day.

FROM LEFT TO RIGHT:
Mom's Pad Woon Cent (opposite),
Mom's Siam Chicken (page 168)

Mom's Siam Chicken

Serves 4

I can say, without a doubt, that you won't find this dish in Thailand—but that doesn't mean it's not worth making! I get a lot of requests for this dish. It marries Thai flavors with a Western approach to Asian cuisine. The "Siam" part of this dish is the use of red curry paste, and the rest of the dish is made of red bell peppers, carrots, and chicken combined into a silky slurry.

- 1 tablespoon cornstarch
- 1 tablespoon neutral oil, such as sunflower
- 2 medium skinless, boneless chicken breast halves (1 pound / 455 g), thinly sliced
- ½ cup (55 g) sliced white onion
- 1 medium carrot, peeled and cut into 2-inch (5 cm) strips
- 2 tablespoons chopped garlic
- 1 medium red bell pepper, sliced
- 1 stalk celery, thinly sliced on the bias
- 1 cup (225 g) sliced water chestnuts
- 2 tablespoons oyster sauce
- 2 tablespoons red curry paste
- 1 tablespoon sugar
- 1 tablespoon Magic Powder (aka Asian chicken bouillon)
- 1 cup (240 ml) Nam Sai (Clear Bone Broth, page 178), plus more if needed
- Steamed rice (see page 36), for serving

First, make a cornstarch slurry: Put the cornstarch in a small bowl, add 1 tablespoon water, and whisk to dissolve. Set aside.

Heat the oil in a large skillet over high heat until it shimmers. Add the chicken and sear on all sides until beginning to brown, about 3 minutes. Add the onion, carrot, and garlic and cook until the vegetables are softened and the garlic is fragrant, about 2 minutes. Add the red pepper, celery, water chestnuts, oyster sauce, red curry paste, sugar, and magic powder and toss to evenly combine. Add the nam sai and bring to a simmer. While stirring, slowly drizzle in just enough cornstarch slurry to thicken the sauce, about 1 minute. Add more nam sai (or water) to loosen the sauce if it becomes too thick.

Transfer to a platter and serve with warm rice. Store leftovers in an airtight container in the refrigerator for up to 3 days.

Phet Palloh

Duck Soy and Five-Spice Stew

Serves 6

Palloh is a style of stew or soup that is a cafeteria classic and childhood favorite in Thailand. It was influenced by Chinese settlers in Bangkok and prominently features star anise, five-spice, sweet soy sauce, and sugar. Kai palloh, which is the most common version of this dish, is typically prepared with boiled eggs and pork belly or pork shoulder, but I've found it pairs well with an array of different proteins. In my version, I swap out the pork with duck; its gamey flavors marry so well with the sticky and syrupy flavor of the sweet soy sauce and sugar. I've also used beef chuck before with incredible results; the meat breaks down into tender bites and absorbs all the palloh flavor and color. You can pick whichever route you want to go down because the technique is the same. And if you really want to go the extra mile, do what I do at the restaurant and smoke the meat for forty-five minutes to an hour over applewood or your favorite wood chips. The time in the smoker adds an entirely new dimension of flavor that foils the sweet soy sauce beautifully.

For the duck:

1 tablespoon neutral oil, such as sunflower

6 duck legs (2½ to 3 pounds / 1.3 kg)

2 stalks celery, halved

½ white onion, quartered

4 (1-inch / 2.5 cm) pieces fresh ginger, unpeeled, sliced (4 ounces / 115 g)

½ bunch fresh cilantro stems

1 (2-ounce / 55 g) disk palm sugar

¼ cup (60 ml) sweet soy sauce

¼ cup (60 ml) oyster sauce

1 teaspoon black peppercorns

2 star anise

1 teaspoon salt

½ teaspoon ground white pepper

½ teaspoon Chinese five-spice powder

For the stew:

¼ cup (30 g) cornstarch

6 hard-cooked eggs

1 package (7.8 ounce / 220 g) fried tofu, cut into 8 pieces (see Note)

For serving:

Fresh cilantro leaves

Thinly sliced scallions, green parts

Pickled mustard greens (store-bought)

Prik Nam Som (Chile Vinegar, page 54)

Steamed rice (see page 36)

(Recipe continues)

MAKE THE DUCK:

Preheat the oven to 250°F (120°C).

In a large braising pot or oval Dutch oven with a lid, heat the oil over medium-high heat until it shimmers. Working in batches, if necessary, add the duck legs, skin-side down, and cook, without moving, until the duck fat renders and the skin starts to turn golden, 4 to 5 minutes.

Add the celery, onion, ginger, cilantro stems, palm sugar, sweet soy sauce, oyster sauce, black peppercorns, star anise, salt, white pepper, five-spice powder, and just enough water to cover the duck legs. Bring the liquid to a rolling boil. Reduce the heat to maintain a simmer and cook for 10 minutes.

Cover the pot and transfer to the oven. Cook until the duck legs are tender, about 2 hours. Using tongs, remove the duck legs to rest on a baking pan. Using a fine-mesh sieve, strain and reserve the liquid. Skim off any fat on the top if serving right away, or let the fat solidify overnight and remove before reheating.

MAKE THE STEW:

Make a cornstarch slurry: Put the cornstarch in a medium bowl, add ¼ cup (60 ml) water, and whisk to dissolve. Set aside.

Return the braising liquid to a saucepan and add the hard-cooked eggs and fried tofu. Simmer over low heat until the eggs begin to turn a light brown color, about 20 minutes. Thicken the liquid using the cornstarch slurry, stirring in 1 tablespoon at a time, until it reaches the consistency of a jus or light syrup.

TO SERVE:

Place a rack in the center of the oven and preheat the broiler.

Place the reserved duck legs on a baking pan, transfer to the oven, and broil for 1 minute.

Ladle the eggs and tofu into serving bowls and place the warm duck legs on top of each. Drizzle the reduced liquid on top and garnish with cilantro and scallions. Serve immediately with pickled mustard greens, prik nam som, and steamed rice. Store leftovers in an airtight container in the refrigerator for up to 3 days.

Note: If store-bought fried tofu is unavailable, use 1 (8 ounce / 227 g) package firm tofu, drained and pressed between two paper towel–lined plates, dried very well, and cut into 8 pieces. Deep- or shallow-fry in hot oil (375°F / 190°C), carefully turning, until crisp and lightly browned, about 5 minutes. Drain on a paper towel–lined plate.

Shrimp and Pineapple Curry

Serves 4

The pineapple in Thailand is some of the sweetest you'll ever taste. They're a lot smaller than pineapples you'll typically find at an American grocery store, and they have a vibrant golden hue and nectar-like flavor that is fabulous on its own, but even more delicious inside a red curry. Although the pineapples stateside are not as sweet, they can still be dressed to impress with the right ingredients. I love to pair pineapple with shrimp for a tropical vibe—the sweetness of the pineapple with the coconut milk is a welcome foil to tart tamarind, spicy chile jam, and herbaceous makrut lime leaves. This dish comes together in a single pot, you only need a few minutes, and the results will wow anyone.

2 tablespoons neutral oil, such as sunflower

8 ounces (225 g) large shrimp, shelled and deveined

12 medium chunks fresh or canned pineapple (3 ounces / 85 g)

¼ cup (30 g) sliced white onion

½ cup (120 ml) coconut milk

2 tablespoons nam prik pao (roasted chile jam)

1 tablespoon red curry paste

6 whole dried Thai chiles

3 fresh makrut lime leaves

½ cup (120 ml) Nam Sai (Clear Bone Broth, page 178)

1½ teaspoons fish sauce

1 tablespoon tamarind concentrate

1 teaspoon sugar

½ cup (53 g) sliced red bell pepper

For serving:

1 Fresno chile, thinly sliced

4 fresh makrut lime leaves, ribs removed and thinly sliced

24 fresh cilantro leaves

Steamed rice (see page 36)

In a large, high-sided sauté pan, heat the oil over medium heat. Add the shrimp, pineapple, and onion and cook, stirring occasionally, until the shrimp begins to turn opaque and the onions start to sweat, about 3 minutes.

Push the shrimp mixture to one side of the pan. Add 2 tablespoons of the coconut milk, the nam prik pao, red curry paste, Thai chiles, and lime leaves and stir to combine. Cook until the curry paste become fragrant, about 1 minute. Add ¼ cup of the coconut milk, the nam sai, fish sauce, tamarind concentrate, and sugar and fold in the shrimp mixture from the side of the pan. Add the red pepper and simmer until the shrimp is fully cooked, about 2 minutes.

TO SERVE:

Transfer to a large serving bowl and drizzle in the remaining 2 tablespoons coconut milk. (There is no need to fully incorporate the coconut milk. This will give a really cool swirly effect to the dish.) Garnish with a scattering of Fresno chiles, the lime leaves, and cilantro. Serve immediately with warm rice. Store leftovers in an airtight container in the refrigerator for up to 3 days.

Green Curry Mussels

Serves 4

I know many people are intimidated by cooking mussels, but I'm here to assure you it's both easy and well worth it to make this green curry at home. The main thing is to clean your mussels thoroughly (see the note on page 118 for more tips). From there, the green curry does a lot of heavy lifting and the mussels, which add their beautiful, briny juices into the curry, turn this into a dish so spectacular and stunning you are sure to impress even the most discerning dinner party guests. Although this is in the "with rice" chapter, and you should definitely eat this dish with steamed white rice, I encourage sopping up the delicate broth with crusty bread as well.

- 2 tablespoons green curry paste
- 1 cup (240 ml) coconut milk
- ¼ white onion, thinly sliced
- ½ green bell pepper, thinly sliced
- 2 ounces (55 g) bamboo shoot strips, prepared per the instructions on page 18 (½ cup)
- 1 pound (455 g) mussels, scrubbed and debearded, preferably PEI
- 1 tablespoon fish sauce
- 1 tablespoon sugar
- 4 green Thai eggplants, cut into quarters (or sub green tomatoes)
- ½ cup (120 ml) Nam Sai (Clear Bone Broth, page 178)

For serving:

- Fresh Thai basil, hand ripped
- Toasted baguette slices (or toast points)
- Steamed rice (see page 36)

In a large, high-sided sauté pan with a lid, combine the green curry paste and 2 tablespoons of the coconut milk and cook over medium-high heat, stirring, until fragrant, about 1 minute. Add the onion, green pepper, bamboo shoots, and mussels and cook for 1 minute. Add the fish sauce, sugar, Thai eggplants, and nam sai, cover, and cook until the mussels pop open, about 4 minutes. Discard any mussels that do not open. Stir in the remaining coconut milk.

TO SERVE:

Transfer to a serving bowl, top with the Thai basil, and serve immediately with toasted bread and steamed rice.

Pull on some fuzzy socks and a giant sweater because it's about to get cozy. Some people misconstrue Thai soups as only fiery and zippy because tom yum is their only connection to Thai soups. It's exactly why I decided not to include a tom yum recipe in this book; although tom yum, the spicy and sour lemongrass soup, is unabashedly delicious and a cherished part of the Thai soup canon, Thai soups can be incredibly delicate and healing, too. I want to celebrate the side of Thai soups that is often overlooked. Take my daikon broth (page 182), for example, which is sweetened only with the subtle flavors of celery and radish, or my mom's rice soup (page 188), which I swear can cure any cold. And there will also be a spicy favorite known as poh thaak (page 184), too, for anyone looking for the flavors of tom yum but in an entirely different dish. I'm here to show you how much range Thai soups really have.

Nam Sai
Clear Bone Broth

Makes 3 quarts (2.8 L)

This recipe is a hug in a bowl—definitely Thailand's version of chicken soup that you eat when you're sick. Like all good broth, it begins with tons of garlic, aromatics, and a chicken carcass. Once you've simmered the broth down, you can get creative. Add noodles of your choice if you want a noodle soup (I love thin rice noodles for this), garlic oil (see my recipe on page 65), a generous shake of white pepper, and a sprinkling of cilantro. You can include shredded chicken if you have it and customize this further with chile vinegar or a bit of sugar. Nothing is more soothing on a cold day than this broth—but it hits on a hot day, too. Thais love to eat soup even in the hottest weather; by raising your internal temperature, you supposedly get the impression that the notoriously hot and humid climate of the country isn't that bad. Whatever the case, make this broth for any season.

- 1 chicken carcass (about 3 pounds / 1.4 kg)
- ½ white onion, peeled and cut into quarters
- 2 stalks celery, cut into large pieces
- ½ bunch fresh cilantro stems
- 5 cloves garlic, unpeeled and cut in half
- 2 tablespoons coriander seeds
- 2 tablespoons kosher salt
- 1 tablespoon salted preserved cabbage
- 1 tablespoon white peppercorns

In a large stockpot, combine the chicken carcass, onion, celery, cilantro stems, garlic, coriander seeds, salt, preserved cabbage, white peppercorns, and 5 quarts (4.7 L) water and bring to a simmer over medium-high heat (do not bring the broth to a boil to prevent a murky broth). Lower the heat to maintain a simmer and simmer, uncovered, for 2 hours.

Strain the broth through a fine-mesh sieve into airtight containers and refrigerate until completely cooled. Skim and discard the fat layer that sets on the top. Cover and refrigerate the broth for up to 4 days or freeze for up to 6 months.

Gaeng Jeud

Clear Soup ("Bland Soup")

Serves 4

Gaeng jeud directly translates to "bland soup." I know, I know—that might not get you super-excited to cook this, but I can assure you that this recipe is anything but bland. Sure, it might not be as spicy or garlicky as some of the other dishes in this book, but what this dish has is nuance and delicate layers of flavor. If you close your eyes and sip, you can taste the sweetness of the chicken broth, a peppery note from cilantro roots, and a gentle vegetal aroma from cilantro and radish. Although the soup can be finished with just cubed daikon and chopped napa cabbage and sipped on as a side dish, Thais like to transform this healing broth into a full meal by adding soft tofu, glass noodles, or whatever they have on hand. I've shared my favorite version, which features pork meatballs, here. If there's someone in your life who wants to try Thai food but is intimidated by the heat, this is the dish to make for them.

For the meatballs:

- 1 pound (455 g) ground pork
- 1 tablespoon chopped garlic
- 2 tablespoons chopped fresh cilantro
- 1 scallion, green and white parts, thinly sliced
- 1 teaspoon Thai seasoning sauce
- 1 tablespoon oyster sauce
- ½ teaspoon ground white pepper

For the broth:

- 2 quarts (2 L) Nam Sai (Clear Bone Broth, page 178)
- 6 cloves garlic, smashed and peeled
- 1 tablespoon preserved salted cabbage
- ¼ bunch fresh cilantro stems, leaves reserved for serving
- 1 (1 pound / 455 g) daikon radish, peeled, halved, and cut into ¼-inch (6 mm) slices (about 3 cups)
- ½ teaspoon ground white pepper
- 1½ teaspoons kosher salt

For serving:

- 2 scallions, green and white parts, cut into 1-inch (2.5 cm) pieces

MAKE THE MEATBALL MIXTURE:

In a large bowl, combine the pork, garlic, cilantro, scallion, seasoning sauce, oyster sauce, and white pepper. Let stand at room temperature while you prepare the broth.

MAKE THE BROTH:

In a large saucepan, combine the nam sai, garlic, salted cabbage, cilantro, daikon, white pepper, and salt and bring to a simmer over medium heat. Continue to simmer until the daikon is just fork tender, like potatoes for potato salad, about 4 minutes.

FINISH THE SOUP:

Using a tablespoon, make a meatball by scooping out some of the pork mixture and then gently lowering it into the simmering broth. Repeat with the remaining meatball mixture. You should have about 20 meatballs. Cook, being careful not to let the broth boil (to avoid the meatballs breaking and clouding the liquid), gently stirring occasionally, until the meatballs float to the top and the internal temperature reads 165°F (75°C), 10 to 12 minutes. Season with additional salt to your taste.

TO SERVE:

Divide the soup among 4 bowls, top with the scallions and cilantro leaves, and serve immediately. Store leftovers in an airtight container in the refrigerator for up to 4 days.

Daikon Broth

Vegan Soup Base

Makes 3 quarts (2.8 L)

Perfect this daikon broth because it is the backbone to several recipes in this chapter, and it's also the ideal thing to sip on a cold day. This soup is unfussy, easy to make, and packed with refined flavor. There are minimal ingredients, which allows the daikon radish to take center stage. The daikon releases so much delicate flavor and is a pleasure to eat. Another bonus is that this elegant broth is vegan. Note that this recipe calls for cilantro stems, not the leaves. In Thai cooking, cilantro stems (or, better yet, the roots) add pepperiness and a depth of flavor. We skip the leaves here because they break down and turn the broth murky.

1 pound (455 g) daikon radish, peeled and cut into large pieces

1 large white onion (460 g), peeled and cut into quarters

2 stalks celery, cut in half

½ bunch fresh cilantro stems

8 cloves garlic, unpeeled and smashed

4 (1-inch / 2.5 cm) pieces fresh ginger (65 g), unpeeled, cut into thick slices

2 tablespoons kosher salt

1 tablespoon sugar

1 teaspoon coriander seeds

1 teaspoon white peppercorns

In a 7-quart (6.6 L) stockpot, combine the radish, onion, celery, cilantro stems, garlic, ginger, salt, sugar, coriander, white peppercorns, and 4 quarts (3.8 L) water and bring to a simmer over medium-high heat. Lower the heat to maintain a simmer and simmer, uncovered, for 45 minutes. (Simmering instead of boiling helps prevent the liquid from becoming murky.)

Cool completely, then strain the broth through a fine-mesh sieve. Cover and refrigerate the broth for up to 5 days or freeze for up to 6 months.

DAIKON BROTH
DAIKON BROTH

Mushroom Poh Thaak

Shipwreck Spicy Herbaceous Citrus Soup

Serves 6

In Thai, a poh is a type of pontoon or boat that's used for fishing and crabbing. *Thaak* means "to crack," which is why this soup is also often called a shipwreck soup. The idea is that all the shellfish and fish captured on the pontoon crash into this soup. I'm doing a vegetarian-friendly version with mushrooms, but feel free to toss in squid, mussels, and/or shrimp if you'd like!

The flavor profile of this soup is quite similar to tom yum, with plenty of makrut lime and lemongrass, but there's definitely a spicier edge and a distinct peppery, almost licorice-like essence from the Thai basil. Ginger isn't typically used in this soup, but I decided to include it in the daikon broth for some added heat, and it does not disappoint.

- 1 quart (960 ml) Daikon Broth (page 182)
- 2 cups (115 g) sliced mixed mushrooms, such as oyster, beech, or enoki
- 8 ounces (225 g) firm tofu, drained and cut into 1-inch (2.5 cm) cubes
- ¼ cup (28 g) sliced white onion
- 1 tablespoon chopped garlic
- 4 fresh red Thai chiles, split in half
- 2 fresh makrut lime leaves, torn
- 1 stalk lemongrass (2 ounces / 55 g), ends trimmed, tough outer layers removed, cut in half lengthwise, then crosswise into 1-inch (2.5 cm) pieces
- 2 scallions, green and white parts, cut into 1-inch (2.5 cm) pieces
- 12 fresh Thai basil leaves
- 2 tablespoons Thai seasoning sauce
- 2 tablespoons fresh lime juice (about 1 lime)
- Pinch of ground white pepper
- Fresh cilantro leaves, for serving

In a medium saucepan, combine the daikon broth, mushrooms, tofu, onion, garlic, Thai chile, makrut lime leaves, and lemongrass and bring to a simmer over medium heat. Simmer for 3 minutes, then add the scallions, Thai basil, seasoning sauce, lime juice, and white pepper, and stir to combine. Spoon into bowls, top with cilantro leaves, and serve immediately. Store leftovers in an airtight container in the refrigerator for up to 4 days.

Simple Jhok

Rice Porridge (Congee)

Serves 4 to 6

For all my fellow Southerners, I like to think of jhok as Thailand's version of grits. Like most Thai porridges, it's made with rice, but jhok is cooked with broken rice and simmered for so long that the rice breaks down until the texture is akin to a bowl of grits or oatmeal. The older and drier the leftover rice for this, the better. For the most part, jhok is served with garlicky pork meatballs, a dusting of white pepper, matchsticks of ginger, and a poached egg for good measure. My version, which I call simple jhok, is sans pork but with preserved cabbage, which adds a subtle briny pop that balances out the richness of the porridge. Jhok is a standard breakfast, but it's also considered a post-clubbing meal as well as something to eat when you're feeling under the weather, so you can make it pretty much any time of day.

2 cups (280 g) day-old steamed rice (the drier the better)

1 teaspoon Magic Powder (aka Asian chicken bouillon)

1 tablespoon salted preserved cabbage

1 teaspoon kosher salt

In a food processor with the knife blade attached, pulse the day-old rice until broken into small grains the size of coarse grits or couscous, about 10 pulses.

In a large saucepan, bring 1 quart (960 ml) water to simmer over medium heat. Add the pulsed rice and stir to combine. Simmer, constantly stirring (to break up any clumps and so the excess rice starches do not settle on the bottom of the pot and burn), until the rice gradually thickens, 3 to 5 minutes. Reduce the heat to low. Add the magic powder, preserved cabbage, and salt and continue cooking, low and slow, stirring occasionally so the rice doesn't stick to the bottom of the pan and adding additional water, ½ cup (120 ml) at a time, to keep it from becoming too thick, until the consistency becomes creamy and slightly thick like rice cereal, another 25 to 30 minutes. Add up to 1 quart (960 ml) total water (which will make 6 cups / 1.4 L jhok). Serve immediately.

Store leftovers in an airtight container in the refrigerator for up to 3 days.

Mom's Khao Thom

Ginger Rice Soup

Serves 4

In terms of breakfast, you're usually a khao thom person or a jhok person, or to be clearer, you're a rice soup person or a rice porridge person. I think both are great for different occasions: Jhok is my go-to for sopping up a wild night out, while khao thom is a light breakfast that's easy on the stomach. Where jhok is thick like oatmeal, khao thom is much soupier with individual rice grains. This is the recipe my mom made for me whenever I wasn't feeling well. A pot would remain on the stove all week long while I healed. Like my mom, I like my khao thom with plenty of ginger and white pepper. For this recipe, I'm going with shrimp, but you can also add poached fish, shredded chicken, or pork meatballs. If you're not a fan of gooey textures like grits and oatmeal, khao thom is the breakfast soup option for you.

1 quart (960 ml) Nam Sai (Clear Bone Broth, page 178)

1 teaspoon finely chopped, peeled fresh ginger

1 teaspoon preserved salted cabbage

2 tablespoons finely chopped white onion

1 tablespoon thinly sliced lemongrass

6 ounces (170 g) large (21/25) shrimp, shelled, deveined, and cut into 3 pieces (11 large shrimp / 1 cup chopped)

1 teaspoon Magic Powder (aka Asian chicken bouillon)

1 tablespoon fish sauce

1 teaspoon sugar

1 cup (55 g) beech mushrooms, trimmed

1 cup (148 g) cooked jasmine rice

For serving:

Fresh cilantro leaves

Thinly sliced scallions (green and white parts)

Garlic Oil (page 65)

Ground white pepper

In a large saucepan, combine the nam sai, ginger, preserved salted cabbage, onion, and lemongrass and bring to a boil over medium heat. Boil for 1 minute, then reduce the heat to maintain a simmer. Add the shrimp, magic powder, fish sauce, and sugar and cook until the shrimp begins to turn opaque, 1 to 2 minutes. Add the mushrooms and rice and cook until the rice releases its starch to slightly thicken the soup, 1 to 2 minutes.

TO SERVE:

Divide among 4 bowls, garnish with cilantro, scallions, garlic oil, and white pepper, and serve immediately. Store leftovers in an airtight container in the refrigerator for up to 2 days.

Mom's Curry Noodle Soup

Coconut "Indian Noodle" Soup

Serves 4

This was my mom's gateway to what we know as khao soi today. She was lofty and so ahead of her time for wanting to introduce a similar flavor profile to Nashville despite not having access to the long list of ingredients a traditional khao soi requires. To be clear, this is not authentic khao soi. A traditional khao soi takes hours for the flavor to develop and requires a fresh curry paste, as well as pickled mustard greens, freshly fried noodles, and roasted ground chiles for finishing. The term *soi*, which means to cut, refers to the freshly made noodles in traditional khao sois. My mom, ever efficient, called this dish "Indian Noodle" to make it more approachable to her customers. She found shortcuts like canned red curry paste and Madras powder to make a rudimentary version of the beloved curry broth and also opted for rice noodles. Although it's not traditional and can't necessarily be compared to the khao sois you'll find in Northern Thailand, it's pretty easy to recreate, and the payoff is equally fragrant and flavorful.

4 ounces (115 g) packaged flat rice noodles (5 mm) or Fresh Rice Noodles (page 40)

1 cup (240 ml) Nam Sai (Clear Bone Broth, page 178)

1 tablespoon red curry paste

1 tablespoon salted preserved cabbage

½ teaspoon Madras curry powder

1 teaspoon Magic Powder (aka Asian chicken bouillon)

6 ounces (170 g) shredded cooked chicken

1 cup (135 g) bean sprouts

2 stalks gai lan (Chinese broccoli), sliced on the bias

2 cups (480 ml) coconut milk

For serving:

Crushed roasted, unsalted peanuts

Fried Shallots (page 64), or store-bought fried shallots

Fresh cilantro leaves

Chile crisp

Lime cheeks (see page 50)

Put the rice noodles in a large bowl. Pour warm water over them and let stand until soft, 20 to 30 minutes. Drain and set aside. (If using fresh noodles, you can skip this step.)

Fill a medium saucepan three-quarters full with water and bring to a boil over high heat.

Combine the nam sai and red curry paste in a large saucepan. Place over medium-high heat and cook, stirring, until the paste becomes fragrant and the color deepens, about 2 minutes. Add the preserved cabbage, curry powder, and magic powder and simmer for 1 minute. Reduce the heat, add the chicken, and simmer for 1 minute.

Put the bean sprouts in a large soup bowl.

Dip the gai lan into the boiling water and cook for 15 seconds. Using a spider or slotted spoon, remove them and add to the bowl with the bean sprouts.

Dip the rehydrated or fresh rice noodles into the same boiling water and cook for 15 seconds. Using a spider or slotted spoon, remove the noodles and transfer to the soup bowl.

Pour the curried chicken soup over the bean sprouts, gai lan, and noodles in the soup bowl. Stir in the coconut milk (if not serving immediately, wait to add the coconut milk until just before serving).

TO SERVE:

Garnish each bowl with crushed peanuts, fried shallots, and cilantro, and serve immediately with chile crisp and lime cheeks on the side.

(The Value of) Crazy Rich Thai Food

Most of the feedback I receive at International Market from my mother's loyal customers from generations past isn't about my food (which is fabulous, if I do say so myself). It's about my prices.

Some diners cannot fathom paying $19.50 for my version of pad see eiw (page 135)—lovingly called "papp" see eiw because it's made with fresh pappardelle noodles—or handing over $28 for my braised beef version of a Thai waterfall salad (page 207). Nevermind that my papp see eiw also has fresh farm eggs, organic gai lan, and local mushrooms, or that my beef salad is braised for hours until it is fork tender. It seems that there is no hesitation to pay $30 for a fresh pasta dish in an Italian restaurant or steak frites at a French place, but Asian food, for whatever reason, is devalued.

Do you know how many ingredients go into a mortar and pestle full of pounded papaya salad? I know salads, on traditional menus, may be considered just starters, but all of the intricacies of Thai salads should be respected—and priced appropriately. Som thums include fresh palm sugar, dehydrated shrimp, Thai chiles, garlic, and tons of green papaya, which can be difficult to source. In the case of koong chae nam pla, the salad is comprised entirely of fresh seafood. The amount of time it takes to develop flavors should also be taken into consideration.

The same case can be made for soups. Big vats of broth that simmer all day long, disguised by the casual setting of streetside vendors boasting plastic stools and folding tables, hold the stigma of quick and cheap eats. However, in a restaurant with white tablecloths, the same soup is suddenly referred to as consommé and priced to match. Do you see where I'm going with this? It takes the same amount of time, deft knowledge of flavor, and technique to make a soup—whether in chef whites or flip flops.

I feel honored that people want to visit the restaurant and spend their hard-earned cash on my food. It is beyond humbling, but I'm also tired of the notion that because takeout Asian food was once cheap, all Asian food should remain cheap forever. There's this idea that the cheaper an Asian spot is, the more authentic it is (if you don't already know how I feel about the term *authenticity*, read about it on page 13). These stereotypes about Asian cuisine are extremely harmful; with my food, I am trying to combat them, and educate my customers, to the best of my ability. Curry paste alone has close to twenty ingredients. When you think about what else goes into a curry—coconut milk, protein, fresh veggies—you start to realize that Asians have been undercharging for decades in an attempt to remain competitive in the restaurant industry. I don't want to devalue my or my mom's food this way. This is why I set my prices the way I do—I have too much respect for the restaurant, my food, my staff, and my purveyors to charge any less.

There have been more and more conversations about this topic in recent years, and I'm happy to add my voice to the mix.

I want to show the world that anyone can cook Thai food. But I also share the nuances that are required to make each dish not just good but exceptionally delicious. There is a lot of thought that goes into creating balanced flavors and contrasting textures, to getting the best possible result, and certain recipes require patience and technique, too. So as we continue to cook together throughout this book, I want to emphasize how everything should be made with intention and encourage you to source the best-quality ingredients possible for every dish.

CHAPTER 9 ◆ SALADS

I need to start this chapter off with a brief Thai lesson. Among the next several pages, you're going to be seeing the word *yum* a lot. *Yum*, in Thai, is a word that refers to both a salad style and a flavor profile. For something to be a yum, it must possess a level of sourness from limes and heat from chiles. That's why something like tom yum, which is a soup and translates to "boiled sour-spice," is a sour and spicy soup. Most other yums you'll come across identify as salads. Recipes like yum kai daow (an egg salad, page 200) and yum mama (an instant ramen salad, page 202) also possess heat from Thai chiles and an assertive brightness from limes. Next time you go to a Thai restaurant, check out all the different yums on the menu. You'll see that although those dishes are delicious, yum doesn't refer to how tasty they are, but the sour and spicy style of cooking that Thais love. You'll also see that pretty much everything can be a yum if you put your mind to it (e.g., my yum hot dog on page 208).

With that said, not every recipe in this salad chapter is a yum. There are four fundamental categories of Thai salads. In addition to yum, there is thum, laab, and plah. In this chapter, I'll introduce you to all of them and more. I have cucumber achaar for you, which is sweet and pickle-y and doesn't neatly fall into any of these categories, but still makes for a wonderful side dish (page 196). There's a roasted mushroom laab that is deeply savory and earthy (page 210). Salad is often—wrongly—seen as boring, but I'm here to show you that Thai salads are anything but.

Cucumber Achaar

Makes 2 cups (500 g)

Although I put this in the salad chapter, this isn't the type of salad you would eat as an entree, but rather an accompaniment or dip to balance out other dishes. It's why it doesn't neatly fall into the four salad categories I've previously mentioned. Everyone goes crazy for the peanut sauce that comes with satay, the skewered meat street food icon. It is undeniably delicious. But the cucumber relish that also comes with satay is an underrated gem. It provides ample tang from vinegar, bite from red onion, and freshness from the cucumbers to cut through the creamy sweetness of the peanut sauce. This is like peanut butter and jelly to me—you can't have one without the other—and fortunately it's super simple to prepare.

¼ cup (60 ml) Sauce Gai (Sweet Chile Sauce, page 60)

1 English (seedless) cucumber, cut in half lengthwise and sliced (about 11 ounces / 300 g)

¼ cup (50 g) chopped tomato

¼ cup thinly sliced (29 g) red onion

2 tablespoons distilled white vinegar

1 tablespoon sugar

½ teaspoon kosher salt

In a large bowl, combine the sauce gai, cucumber, tomato, onion, vinegar, sugar, and salt. Let stand at room temperature for at least 30 minutes but ideally 2 hours before serving (see Note).

Store in an airtight container in the refrigerator for up to 1 week. The cucumber will pickle slightly, giving it a great texture.

Note: It's great at the 2-hour mark, so if you can wait, do. It's fun to taste it over time as the flavor changes and develops. Keep in mind that the acid from the vinegar will continue to develop and intensify the pickled flavor of the cucumber.

Koong Chae Nam Pla
Shrimp Ceviche

Serves 4

I like to think of this dish as Thailand's version of ceviche. It doesn't fall neatly into any of the aforementioned salad types, but the flavor profile closely resembles a yum. The traditional version of koong chae nam pla calls for raw shrimp beautifully butterflied, accompanied by bitter melon and doused in nam jim talay, the tongue-tingling sauce that Thais eat with seafood—cockles, fish, mussels, lobster, you name it. The lime juice in the seafood sauce helps to cure the shrimp, and the thinly sliced garlic that adorns each shrimp adds even more of a bite. This is a perfect appetizer for a seafood feast, and when arranged strategically, all the colorful aspects of this dish make it a showstopper. At the restaurant, I serve an elevated version as a crudo made with raw scallops or salmon, but for home cooks I wanted to make this dish a bit more approachable by using poached shrimp instead of raw shrimp. Thais eat whole shrimp like these on their own, but I love the crunch of tortilla chips served with them, and their added saltiness works to counteract the acid.

- 6 ounces (170 g) large (21/25) shrimp, shelled, deveined, and split in half lengthwise
- 2 tablespoons chopped white onion
- 2 cloves garlic, thinly sliced
- 1 Fresno chile, thinly sliced
- 1 red radish, thinly sliced
- ¼ cup (60 ml) Nam Jim Talay (Thai Seafood Sauce, page 75)

For serving:

- 12 fresh mint leaves
- Fresh dill sprigs
- Green cabbage wedges
- Cucumber slices
- Store-bought tortilla chips

Make an ice bath: Fill a large bowl with ice and cold water.

Bring a medium saucepan filled with salted water to a boil over high heat. Add the shrimp and cook until opaque, about 1 minute. Using a spider or large slotted spoon, remove and immediately transfer to the ice bath.

In a large bowl, combine the onion, garlic, Fresno chile, radish, and cooked shrimp. Pour the nam jim talay over the shrimp mixture and stir to evenly combine. Cover and refrigerate for 15 minutes to marinate.

TO SERVE:

Just before serving, gently fold in the mint leaves. Transfer to a shallow serving bowl and garnish with dill. Serve with cabbage wedges, cucumber slices, and tortilla chips.

Yum Kai Daow

Fried Egg Salad

Serves 4

When it comes to egg salad, I think of three things: the Japanese sando version, a Southern deviled egg-ish picnic sandwich, and the Thai version—which, of course, I think is the best kind. Yum kai daow is full of bright flavor and craveable, runny, crispy fried eggs. This is one of the simplest dishes to make, and the payoff is enormous. If there was ever a midnight meal—what you make after a long day when you just want something easy, comforting, and undeniably good—it's this. Everyone has their own variation of yum kai daow, but the star here is the kai dao, which means "star egg" in Thai (the equivalent of sunny-side-up eggs). You want gooey centers, lots of shallots and Thai chiles, and other salad ingredients like tomato, celery, and cilantro. When I'm feeling extra-fancy, I spruce mine up with fish roe for a fun egg-on-egg moment. The crunchy edges of the eggs, the burst of the yolk, and the saltiness of fish sauce makes this a heavenly plate at midnight, yes, but also at any other time of day.

For the dressing:

3 tablespoons fresh lime juice

2 tablespoons fish sauce

2 tablespoons chopped fresh cilantro

1 tablespoon minced garlic

½ to 1 teaspoon chopped fresh Thai chile (1 to 2 chiles)

1½ tablespoons sugar

For the salad:

Neutral oil, such as sunflower, for frying (about 1 cup)

6 large eggs

2 stalks Chinese celery (60 g), stalks thinly sliced, leaves separated and kept whole (use American celery if unavailable)

1 large shallot (45 g) (or red onion), halved and thinly sliced

12 grape or cherry tomatoes, halved (about 70 g)

24 fresh cilantro leaves, plus more for garnish

For serving:

Whole fresh red Thai chiles

Ground white pepper

MAKE THE DRESSING:

In a medium bowl, combine the lime juice, fish sauce, cilantro, garlic, Thai chile, and sugar and stir until the sugar is dissolved, about 1 minute. You will have about ½ cup (120 ml). Cover and refrigerate until ready to use.

MAKE THE SALAD:

Pour oil to come ¼ inch (6 mm) up the sides of a large, high-sided skillet and heat over high heat until shimmering. Gently crack the eggs individually into the oil, in batches if necessary, allowing the whites to cook and crisp, about 2 minutes. Once each egg releases from the pan and the yolk is cooked to your desired doneness, using a slotted spoon or spatula, transfer to a wire rack (not a plate or baking pan) and set aside.

In a large bowl, combine the celery, celery leaves, shallot, tomatoes, and cilantro leaves. Pour half the dressing over the mixture and lightly toss to evenly combine.

TO SERVE:

To compose the salad, layer the fried eggs onto a serving platter and drizzle with 1 to 2 tablespoons of the remaining dressing and then top with the salad mixture. Add more dressing, if desired, or serve the remaining dressing in a ramekin on the side. Garnish with whole Thai chiles, cilantro leaves, and a sprinkle of white pepper.

LE CREUSET
LE CREUSET

Yum Mama
Instant Ramen Salad

Serves 4

The idea of an instant ramen salad may seem comical to some, but I promise this salad is no joke and is a celebrated part of Thai cuisine (and a true piece of my own culinary history). In my early twenties, I went on vacation to Thailand with my family. Two days after I returned stateside, I felt an unshakeable call to go back to Thailand. I immediately packed my bags and returned to Thailand's capital. I ended up living in Bangkok for two years! By my apartment in the city, there was a street vendor who set up shop late at night when the pubs began closing. Since I was embracing this youthful the-best-years-of-my-life era, I found myself frequently at his stall in the early, early morning devouring multiple portions of his Mama-brand instant noodle salad. Is there a better meal at 3 a.m.?

If you dress it up the right way, instant ramen is an excellent—and easy!—vehicle for flavor. You can serve this salad warm or cold; the most important thing is to make sure the noodles aren't overcooked or undercooked and to add lots of fresh lime juice, chiles, and herbs, which give the yum its signature tart and spicy flavor.

For the dressing:

- ½ teaspoon Prik Pohn (Toasted Ground Chile, page 54) or crushed dried Thai chile (about 1 chile)
- 1 tablespoon nam prik pao (roasted chile jam)
- 1 tablespoon sugar
- 1 tablespoon fish sauce
- 1½ tablespoons fresh lime juice

For the salad:

- 4 ounces (115 g) ground pork
- 4 ounces (115 g) large shrimp, shelled and deveined
- 4 ounces (115 g) cleaned calamari
- 1 (2.1-ounce / 60 g) packet dried instant ramen, such as Mama, seasoning packet discarded
- 1 Roma tomato (about 5½ ounces / 155 g), cut into 6 wedges
- 1 scallion, green parts, cut into 1-inch (2.5 cm) pieces
- ½ stalk celery, thinly sliced on the bias

For serving:

- Lettuce leaves, such as romaine or green oak leaf
- Fresh cilantro leaves

(Recipe continues)

Fill a large saucepan three-quarters full of water and bring to a rolling simmer over medium heat.

MAKE THE DRESSING:

In a medium bowl, combine the prik pohn, nam prik pao, sugar, fish sauce, and lime juice. Set aside.

MAKE THE SALAD:

Add the ground pork to the simmering water and cook until no longer pink, about 2 minutes. Using a fine-mesh sieve or slotted spoon, transfer to a large bowl. Return the water to a simmer.

Add the shrimp to the same water and cook until opaque, about 2 minutes. Use a spider or slotted spoon to transfer to the bowl with the pork. Return the water to a simmer.

Add the calamari to the simmering water and cook until opaque, 30 seconds to 1 minute. Use the spider or slotted spoon to transfer to the bowl with the pork and shrimp. Return the water to a simmer.

Add the noodles to the same simmering water and cook until tender, about 3 minutes.

Meanwhile, add the tomato, scallion, celery, and dressing to the bowl with the pork, shrimp, and calamari and toss until evenly combined and well coated.

Drain the noodles and transfer to the salad bowl. Toss everything together to combine.

TO SERVE:

Place lettuce leaves on a serving platter and top with the ramen salad. Garnish with cilantro and serve immediately, or if you'd like to serve this cold, reserve the cooked noodles and combine just before serving.

Plah Koong Yang

Spicy Grilled Shrimp Salad

Serves 4

You might know yum, thum, and laab, but there are actually four identities in the world of Thai salad, and this is the fourth. Plah is commonly marked by a stickier, full-bodied dressing that's made from roasted chile jam. It's also very protein-forward. In this instance, the dish is primarily comprised of grilled shrimp. It's not as light or acidic as the yums and thums you may have had, but it's a delicious dish that still feels bright thanks to fresh cilantro, red onion, and vibrant Fresno chiles. I serve my version in lettuce wraps, but it's just as good spooned over fresh steamed rice.

For the dressing:

- 1 tablespoon nam prik pao (roasted chile jam)
- 1 tablespoon fresh lime juice
- 1 teaspoon fish sauce
- ½ teaspoon Magic Powder (aka Asian chicken bouillon)
- 1 tablespoon sugar

For the shrimp:

- 8 ounces (225 g) large (21/25) shrimp, shelled and deveined
- 1 tablespoon neutral oil, such as sunflower
- 1 stalk lemongrass (about 2 ounces / 55 g), ends trimmed, tough outer leaves removed, and thinly sliced
- ¼ cup (30 g) thinly sliced red onion
- 4 makrut lime leaves, ribs removed and thinly sliced
- 1 teaspoon Prik Pohn (Toasted Ground Chile, page 54) or crushed dried Thai chile (about 2 chiles)
- 2 Fresno chiles, thinly sliced

For serving:

- ¼ cup (15 g) Fried Shallots (page 64) or store-bought fried shallots
- 24 fresh cilantro leaves
- Green lettuce leaves, such as romaine or iceberg

MAKE THE DRESSING:

In a medium bowl, combine the nam prik pao, lime juice, fish sauce, magic powder, sugar, and 2 tablespoons water.

MAKE THE SHRIMP:

Set a clean grill to high heat (or use a grill pan over high heat). Using a brush, coat the shrimp with the oil. Carefully lay the shrimp on the hot grill (or grill pan) and grill until lightly seared (you should see it just beginning to brown), about 2 minutes. Flip the shrimp and grill until opaque throughout, being careful not to overcook, another 1 to 2 minutes. Transfer the shrimp to a large bowl.

Add the lemongrass, red onion, makrut lime leaves, prik pohn, and Fresno chile to the bowl with the shrimp. Pour the dressing over the shrimp mixture and toss until evenly coated.

TO SERVE:

Add half of the fried shallots and lightly toss to combine. Garnish with cilantro and the remaining fried shallots. Serve with lettuce leaves.

FROM TOP:
Nam Thok (opposite),
Plah Koon Yang (page 205)

Nam Thok
Waterfall Beef Salad

Serves 4

Nam thok, which means "waterfall," typically refers to the juices that drip from a marbled steak—like a waterfall—when preparing this dish. To achieve exactly what this dish describes, I'm using a beautiful cut of New York strip steak. A rib eye would work well here, too. When you pair this sliced steak with the rest of the salad components—which include fish sauce, lime juice, chiles, and plenty of herbs—you'll never want steak any other way again. Worcestershire what? A.1. who?

- 1 (8-ounce / 225 g) New York strip steak
- Kosher salt and coarsely ground black pepper
- 1 Roma tomato (about 5½ ounces / 155 g), cut into wedges
- ¼ red onion, thinly sliced
- 1 stalk lemongrass (about 2 ounces / 50 g), ends trimmed, tough outer leaves removed, and thinly sliced
- 1 teaspoon Prik Pohn (Toasted Ground Chile, page 54) or crushed dried Thai chile (about 2 chiles)
- 8 fresh cilantro sprigs
- 24 fresh mint leaves
- ¼ cup (60 ml) fresh lime juice
- 2 tablespoons sugar
- 2 tablespoons fish sauce
- 1 tablespoon Khao Kuah (Toasted Rice Powder, page 62)

For serving:

- Nam Jim Jaeow (Dried Chile Sauce, page 72)
- Sticky Rice (page 38)

About 30 to 60 minutes before cooking, remove the steak from the fridge to bring it to room temperature. Pat the steak dry and season with salt and pepper. In a grill pan or cast-iron skillet over medium-high heat, sear the steak until a crispy, brown crust forms, about 5 minutes. Flip and cook to medium rare (when it measures 130°F/ 55°C on an instant-read thermometer), about 7 minutes.

Transfer the steak to a cutting board and let rest for 10 minutes.

Meanwhile, in a large bowl, combine the tomato, onion, lemongrass, prik pohn, cilantro, mint, lime juice, sugar, fish sauce, and khao kuah and stir until the sugar is dissolved.

Thinly slice the steak and gently toss with the tomato mixture to combine.

TO SERVE:

Transfer to a serving platter and serve with nam jim jaeow and sticky rice.

Yum Hot Dog
Hot Dog Salad

Serves 2 to 4

I know what you're thinking: "Hot dog salad?!" And to that I say a resounding *yes*! Look, hot dogs with ketchup and mustard are classic but a bit overplayed. And because hot dogs are so salty, giving them the yum treatment is the perfect way to balance them out. You probably never envisioned finding hot dogs refreshing, but because I'm a magician in the kitchen, I can make that happen for you. The celery leaves, tomatoes, and celery really cut through the salt and fat of the hot dog, making this a dish you should bring to your next cookout—hold the buns.

For the hot dogs:

2 hot dogs sliced on the bias

For the sauce:

¼ cup (60 ml) fresh lime juice

3 tablespoons fish sauce

2 tablespoons sugar

1 teaspoon minced garlic

1 teaspoon chopped fresh Thai chile (about 2 chiles)

For the salad:

¼ medium red onion, sliced

1 stalk celery, thinly sliced on the bias, leaves reserved

6 grape tomatoes, halved

24 fresh cilantro leaves (about ¼ bunch)

8 green leaf lettuce leaves, torn into pieces

MAKE THE HOT DOGS:

Adjust a rack 5 to 6 inches (12 to 15 cm) from your oven's heat source and preheat the broiler. Place the hot dogs on a baking pan in a single layer and broil, flipping the slices halfway through, until lightly roasted, about 4 minutes.

MEANWHILE, MAKE THE SAUCE:

In a small bowl, combine the lime juice, fish sauce, sugar, garlic, and Thai chile. Set aside.

MAKE THE SALAD:

Put the broiled hot dogs, onion, sliced celery, and tomatoes in a large bowl. Pour the sauce over the mixture and toss until well coated. Fold in the celery leaves and cilantro.

TO SERVE:

Divide the lettuce between 2 to 4 plates. Top with the hot dog salad and drizzle any remaining sauce in the bottom of the bowl over the top. Serve immediately.

Roasted Mushroom Laab

Mushroom Salad

Serves 4

Laab, a northeastern Thai dish with roots in Laos, can be made from pretty much anything. The main thing to keep in mind, what makes a laab truly a laab, is the combination of herbs and aromatics (mint, shallots or red onion, cilantro, and toasted rice powder cannot be omitted). Traditionalists will typically use ground pork or chicken, but I've also seen laab made with duck and salmon. I also like to do this plant-based riff with roasted mushrooms (withhold magic powder, or use a veg-friendly version, if you want to make this dish fully vegetarian). You can use any combination you like. My favorites are oyster and trumpet, but feel free to pull out the maitake or shiitake, too! The earthy, umami notes from the mushrooms are a wonderful foil to zingy lime juice, toasty rice powder, herbaceous mint, and the heat from Thai chiles. And, yes, it's pronounced *laab* like you're saying "ahhh!" at the dentist's office and not *larb* like *barb*.

For the mushrooms:

6 ounces (170 g) mixed heirloom mushrooms, such as oyster, trumpet, and/or maitake, trimmed and ripped into large, even pieces (about 2 cups)

For the dressing:

2 tablespoons vinegar from Pickled Garlic and Vinegar (page 62)

1 tablespoon fresh lime juice

2 tablespoons Thai seasoning sauce

1½ teaspoons Prik Pohn (Toasted Ground Chile, page 54) or crushed dried Thai chile (about 3 chiles), plus more for serving

1 tablespoon sugar

1½ teaspoons Magic Powder (aka Asian chicken bouillon)

For the laab:

¼ cup (30 g) thinly sliced red onion

2 tablespoons sliced lemongrass (ends trimmed, tough outer leaves removed, and sliced into thin rounds)

1 tablespoon Pickled Garlic (page 62)

For serving:

1 teaspoon Khao Kuah (Toasted Rice Powder, page 62)

24 fresh mint leaves

12 fresh cilantro leaves

Fresh dill sprigs

Thinly sliced green cabbage

MAKE THE MUSHROOMS:

Adjust a rack 5 to 6 inches (12 to 15 cm) from your oven's heat source and preheat the broiler to low. Arrange the mushrooms on a baking pan in a single layer and place under the broiler. Broil until slightly dried out and charred, about 6 minutes.

MEANWHILE, MAKE THE DRESSING:

In a small bowl, whisk the vinegar, lime juice, Thai seasoning sauce, prik pohn, sugar, and magic powder until evenly combined.

FINISH THE LAAB:

In a large bowl, combine the red onion, lemongrass, pickled garlic, and roasted mushrooms. Pour the dressing over the mushroom mixture and, using a spatula, mix until combined and well coated with the dressing.

TO SERVE:

Sprinkle the khao kuah over the mixture and gently fold in the mint, cilantro, and dill. Serve immediately on a bed of thinly sliced cabbage and sprinkle prik pohn over the top, if desired.

Som Thum Tua
Green Bean Salad

Serves 2 to 4

When you see som thum on a menu, you might think of the classic Thai green papaya salad. But many people don't realize that you can "thum," or pound, anything into a version of papaya salad (minus the papaya). There's thum thang, or spicy cucumber salad, and thum carrot, which is a great alternative to papaya when you can't find it. My go-to version is thum tua, or green bean salad. The heartiness of green beans and the slightly bitter flavor plays perfectly with the fish sauce, lime, garlic, and chiles of a traditional papaya salad. I find that the beans absorb the sauce well and maintain ample crunch, which is important for a dish that requires so much pounding. I'd almost argue that it's better than the original papaya version, or, at the very least, heartier.

- 2 tablespoons dried shrimp
- 2 cloves garlic, peeled
- 1 to 4 fresh red Thai chiles, depending on spice preference
- ½ (2-ounce / 55 g) disk palm sugar, cut into quarters, plus more for serving
- 5 grape tomatoes, halved
- 2 limes, skin on, cut into cheeks (see Note), plus more for serving
- ½ pound (225 g) green beans, trimmed and cut into 1-inch (2.5 cm) pieces
- 2 tablespoons fish sauce, plus more for serving
- 2 tablespoons roasted, unsalted peanuts

In a large mortar with pestle, pound the dried shrimp, garlic, Thai chiles, and palm sugar until a paste begins to form, about 2 minutes. Add the tomatoes and 4 skin-on lime cheeks and continue to pound the ingredients together for 1 to 2 minutes (to prevent splashing, cover the mortar with a kitchen towel). Add one-quarter of the green beans and the fish sauce. Squeeze in the juice of 2 lime cheeks (about 1 to 2 tablespoons lime juice) and discard the peels in the mortar. Continue to pound the ingredients until the green beans break down slightly, 3 to 4 minutes. At this point, there should be a significant amount of juice.

Repeat the process with the remaining green beans, in batches, if necessary. After you pound the last batch of green beans in the mortar, add the peanuts and lightly crush them, keeping in mind that overgrinding the peanuts will give the salad a mealy texture. Stir to evenly incorporate the peanuts into the salad and season with additional lime juice, fish sauce, and palm sugar, if desired.

Transfer to a serving bowl and serve immediately.

Note: Instead of merely using the lime juice for this salad, Thais tend to toss the whole lime cheek inside. This is not only to keep with tradition, but to add depth of flavor. Though inedible, the lime skin's oils and bitterness from the zest deepen and punctuate the brightness of the salad.

TIPAROS
FISH SAUCE

Mama Myint: Matriarch of Belmont Boulevard

On a rare Sunday funday I found myself at a local Nashville gay bar having a nightcap with my bestie Sutan, aka Raja (yes, the drag queen), who was visiting for my daughter's birthday. We first met when he won his season of *Drag Race*, and I was on *Top Chef*.

It's inevitable that when we are out, a fan approaches him for a chat and photo. He is gracious and always obliges their requests; this particular evening, it was no different. A young man began chatting with Sutan while his female companion started talking to me. Somehow, the conversation shifted to what I do for work, and a light bulb seemed to appear above the woman's face. "Wait, is your mom Mrs. Patti?" she asked. "I was a student at Belmont and left flowers at the front of her restaurant when she passed. Everyone loved her."

I learned that the woman, McKenzie, was adopted from Korea at eight months of age. Growing up, her Asian-ness was seldom discussed or embraced; she remarked that she believed she was white until her teenage years and described her relationship with food being one where salt was an exotic ingredient. She attended the university adjacent to International Market, a music-focused Baptist school, which attracts an eclectic mix of misfits and aspiring artists. It was only then, as a clarinet music major (turned neuroscientist) during her freshman year, that she began to explore her roots and discover a new world of flavor from my mother.

"I had never had actual authentic, real Asian food," McKenzie reminisced. "And your mom decided to make me an order of pad Thai with chicken and did not charge me for it." McKenzie went on to describe the transcendent experience of eating my mom's food that day, and the feeling of validation she received enjoying Asian food that she had never been exposed to prior, despite her ethnic background. She felt seen by my mom, someone who also looked like her.

It made me think about my mom's persevering warmth, how years after her passing I can still run into people who have such fond memories of her food, yes, but also her kindness and welcoming nature. There are so many people who have been touched by my mom's generosity, and it always feels like a wave from her when I get to hear these stories for the first time. McKenzie emphasized that everyone at Belmont, not just her, saw my mom as a maternal figure known for taking people in and feeding them, often for free. In fact, she had packed McKenzie boxes of freshly cooked pad Thai during finals week, when she had run out of dining credit and couldn't afford to feed herself.

My mom never did these things with the expectation that she would get paid back for it (although McKenzie did tell me she worked hard throughout her college years in the hopes of being able to show her appreciation to my mom in the future). She was raised Buddhist, and so much of her lifestyle was based in caring for others and providing for those who have less. These are the philosophies she has also instilled in me; it's why I make it a point to volunteer with the Nashville Food Project, Nashville Cares, Nashville Launch Pad, and other non-profit organizations. It had never occurred to me that this was behavior I learned from my mother until I talked to McKenzie—it just felt second nature to me. I now realize that I do the things I do because I had the best example right in front of me: my mom, sharing a meal with a friend or stranger at a table that welcomed all.

SINGHA
SODA WATER

The term "family meal" means so many different things to me. It, of course, reminds me of my mom and dad and my sister and all the magical meals we shared in my childhood. It reminds me of my International Market family, both new and old, and the food we share and bond over before service. It also makes me think of my daughter, Henley, and the way I want her to grow up with the spectacular meals my mom once made me with dozens of accoutrements and side dishes. Will Henley love her jhok with extra ginger and white pepper, like me, or prefer her shrimp paste rice with an absurd amount of sweet pork? Will she want to load up her vermicelli curry with fish balls, or choose sweet soy over chile garlic when it comes to saucing her khao mahn gai? Whatever the case, I'm excited to cook these brilliant, expansive meals for her, and show you how to make these in your own home, too.

Patti's House Salad

Mom's Interactive Lettuce Wraps

Serves 4

My mom's salad is an International Market icon. Despite being on my mom's secret menu (a selection of unabashedly Thai dishes my mom offered only to customers in-the-know), people all over Nashville discovered this salad and whispered about it to friends and neighbors alike. Like a salad shaman, I remember my mom guiding every participant in the art of eating this salad, first insisting that everyone wash their hands before instructing diners to "put only one of everything into the leaf, then put it all in your mouth. Just one bite." The singular bite is crucial to the experience of enjoying this wrap, a flavor and textural explosion. After that initial bite, Mom would leave her guests to build their own euphoric adventure.

The popularity of this salad platter has only continued to grow since my mom first quietly made it for guests. Based on a traditional Thai dish called *miang kham* (essentially a betel leaf wrap), this is a glorified take and an experience in and of itself. It's a wonderland of accoutrements—from spicy red onions to roasted peanuts to slivers of gingery pork—intended to be fully customized into bite-size wraps. Although betel leaves are traditional, I use lettuce as it's easier to source and its neutral flavor is more of a blank canvas. There's so much going on in this salad. The flavors range from sweet to nutty to spicy and sour. There's bite, there's texture, there's both freshness and funkiness. Customers love that they can load up on their favorites, whether it's extra toasted coconut or submerging their wraps in a blanket of tangy tamarind sauce. Whatever kind of wrap you create, make sure you eat everything in a single bite, close your eyes, and taste it all.

For the pork:

- 1 tablespoon neutral oil, such as sunflower
- ¼ cup (30 g) chopped white onion
- 1 teaspoon finely chopped garlic
- 1 teaspoon finely chopped, peeled fresh ginger
- 8 ounces (225 g) boneless pork shoulder, trimmed, thinly sliced, and cut into 1-inch (2.5 cm) squares
- 1½ tablespoons sugar
- 1 tablespoon fish sauce
- 1 tablespoon Thai seasoning sauce
- 2 tablespoons chopped preserved sweet radish

For the salad platter:

- ¼ cup (30 g) chopped red onion
- ¼ cup (40 g) chopped lime (skin on)
- ¼ cup (35 g) roasted, unsalted peanuts
- ¼ cup (15 g) thinly sliced lemongrass (trimmed and tough outer leaves removed)
- ¼ cup (35 g) Pickled Garlic (page 62)
- ¼ cup (35 g) sweet preserved radish
- ¼ cup (30 g) chopped green beans (1-inch / 2.5 cm pieces)
- ¼ cup (15 g) Fried Shallots (page 64), or store-bought fried shallots
- ¼ cup (20 g) toasted unsweetened shredded coconut (see Note, page 220)
- ¼ cup (25 g) chopped fresh red Thai chiles
- ¼ cup (15 g) fresh cilantro leaves
- ¼ cup (10 g) fresh Thai basil leaves
- Lettuce leaves, such as green leaf or romaine
- Cooked rice vermicelli noodles, chilled
- Tamarind Sauce (page 58)

(Recipe continues)

MAKE THE PORK:

Heat the oil in a large skillet over medium-high heat. Add the onion, garlic, and ginger and cook until the onion is translucent and fragrant, about 1 minute. Add the pork and cook on one side, about 2 minutes. Using tongs, flip the pork and add the sugar, fish sauce, and Thai seasoning sauce. Cook, stirring, until the pork begins to caramelize and is cooked through, about 2 minutes. Add the sweet preserved radish and toss to combine. Transfer to a serving bowl and set aside.

MAKE THE SALAD PLATTER:

Place the bowl with the pork in the center of a large serving platter and surround it with ramekins containing the red onion, lime, peanuts, lemongrass, pickled garlic, preserved radish, green beans, fried shallots, coconut, Thai chiles, cilantro, and Thai basil. On a separate plate, lay the lettuce leaves next to a pile of noodles and a ramekin of the tamarind sauce.

TO EAT:

Build a lettuce wrap bite by topping a lettuce leaf with noodles, a pinch of pork, and then a small amount of each accoutrement. Fold and bite!

Note: To toast the coconut: In a dry medium skillet, toast the coconut over medium heat until pale golden brown, 2 to 3 minutes. Transfer to a bowl and set aside.

Jhok Platter

Congee with Accoutrements

Serves 4

You might not think of congee as a thrilling centerpiece like an entire fried chicken showered with fried shallots or a vat of curry. But, to me, jhok with accoutrements is one of the most comforting—and unassumingly delicious—meals you can have. I like my jhok seasoned simply with salt and accompanied by a platter of flavorful sides: tart pickled mustard greens, shredded ginger, ribbons of omelet, sweet sausage, and pork floss are some of my favorites. The jhok is the common thread that holds the complex flavors of the side dishes together. I love how much texture can be found in this meal, from the creaminess of the broken-down rice to the gentle sweetness and bite of the radish omelet and the crunch of fried tofu. Think of this dish as a savory and comforting sundae bar that's great for a weekend breakfast or a late-night bite, a favorite of partygoers in Bangkok and LA's Thai Town.

For the sweet radish omelet:

3 large eggs

1 teaspoon fish sauce

½ teaspoon sugar

½ teaspoon Magic Powder (aka chicken bouillon)

Pinch of ground white pepper

1 tablespoon chopped preserved sweet radish

8 slices white onion

2 tablespoons neutral oil, such as sunflower

For the fried tofu croutons:

1 (14-ounce / 400 g) package firm tofu, drained

Neutral oil, such as sunflower, for frying (about 6 cups / 1.4 L)

For the platter:

4 cups (960 ml) Simple Jhok (Rice Porridge, page 186)

¼ cup (30 g) cooked sweet Chinese sausage, thinly sliced

¼ cup (20 g) peeled fresh ginger, cut into thin strips

¼ cup (20 g) thinly sliced scallions, green and white parts

¼ cup (10 g) pork floss

¼ cup (30 g) pickled mustard greens

Thai seasoning sauce

Chile crisp

Ground white pepper

(Recipe continues)

MAKE THE SWEET RADISH OMELET:

Preheat the oven to 350°F (175°C).

In a large bowl, beat the eggs, fish sauce, sugar, magic powder, and white pepper with a wire whisk. Using a rubber spatula, fold in the preserved radish and onion until evenly combined.

In an oven-safe nonstick 8-inch (20 cm) skillet, heat the oil over high heat until it shimmers. Gently pour in the omelet batter. As the egg begins to set, use the spatula to pull the edges of the omelet toward the center and let the egg run underneath. Continue pulling until the bottom of the eggs are set but the surface is still runny, about 2 minutes. Carefully flip the omelet in the pan, using a spatula like you would flip a pancake, and cook until both sides of the omelet are golden brown and the edges are crispy, another 1 to 2 minutes.

Transfer the pan to the oven and cook until deep brown and crispy, about 5 minutes. Cool, then cut into 1-inch (2.5 cm) squares.

MAKE THE TOFU CROUTONS:

Using paper towels, pat the tofu until very dry and cut into ¾-inch (2 cm) cubes.

Pour oil to come 1½ inches (4 cm) up the sides of a deep saucepan and heat over medium heat until a deep-fry thermometer reads 375°F (190°C). Add the tofu, in batches if necessary so the tofu has enough room to dance, and cook, gently moving the tofu to keep it from sticking to the edges or bottom of the pan, until the exterior is golden brown, about 5 minutes. Using a spider or slotted spoon, transfer to a paper towel–lined plate to drain excess oil. Set aside.

ASSEMBLE THE PLATTER:

Reheat the jhok in a large saucepan, adding up to ¼ cup (60 ml) water, if needed, to loosen the rice.

In a small skillet over medium heat, cook the sausage for 1 to 2 minutes, lightly tossing until the oils release and the color of the sausage deepens from pink to red. Set aside.

Transfer the warm jhok into a large bowl (or 4 individual soup bowls). Surround the jhok with small ramekins filled with the sweet radish egg omelet squares, fried tofu croutons, Chinese sausage, ginger, scallions, pork floss, and pickled mustard greens to sprinkle onto your bowl of jhok as you like. Season with Thai seasoning sauce, chile crisp, and white pepper.

NET WEIGHT

Cha-Om Omelet, Mackerel, and Grapi

Stinky Herb Omelet, Fried Cured Mackerel, and Funky Shrimp Paste Dip

Makes 1 (8-inch / 20 cm) omelet; serves 4

I've had people ask me, "What do Thais *really* eat at home?" This is the answer. I can't think of an ensemble that resembles Thai home cooking more than this bitter and aggressively funky cha-om omelet, a fried salt-cured mackerel, and shrimp paste dip to top it all off. This, alongside a steaming hot bowl of rice, is the pinnacle of Thai home cooking. The brininess of the shrimp paste balances the pungent scent of cha-om and is mellowed out by perfectly fried, flaky mackerel. It's the most classic combination and one of my favorite meals to make and eat. In certain seasons, cha-om is available fresh in the produce section of Asian markets. However, the vacuum-sealed frozen version still delivers on cha-om's distinct promise and lingering attributes. Cha-om, or acacia leaves, have a one-of-a-kind smell when raw that many people find off-putting, but it is reduced by cooking. They have a flavor that many of us can't resist—bitter, herbaceous, and nutty. Go on, give it a try! Keep in mind that when working with this herb there are thorns on the stems, so be cautious when removing the fronds.

For the mackerel:

About 1 cup (240 ml) neutral oil, such as sunflower, for frying

1 (9-ounce / 255 g) package steamed, cured mackerel from the Asian market (2 mackerel), defrosted

For the omelet:

4 ounces (115 g) cha-om (acacia leaves) from 1 (8-ounce / 225 g) package from the Asian market, defrosted if frozen, plus more for serving

3 large eggs

1 teaspoon fish sauce

⅛ teaspoon ground white pepper

¼ teaspoon Magic Powder (aka Asian chicken bouillon)

2 tablespoons neutral oil, such as sunflower

For serving:

Nam Prik Grapi (Shrimp Paste Chile Dip, page 74)

Steamed rice (see page 36)

Fresh cilantro sprigs

Pork rinds

Sliced cucumber

Cabbage wedges

Fresh red Thai chiles

Thai eggplants

Turkey berry eggplants

Green beans

(Recipe continues)

MAKE THE MACKEREL:

Pour oil to come ½ inch (12 mm) up the sides of a large, high-sided skillet. Heat over medium-high heat until simmering. Carefully lay the mackerel down in the pan away from you to avoid any oil splashes and cook, flipping once, until the outer skin is golden, about 6 minutes. (Alternatively, you can deep-fry the mackerel.)

MAKE THE OMELET:

Carefully remove the cha-om leaves from the stems using your hands, being cautious of the small thorns.

In a large bowl, combine the cha-om leaves with the eggs, fish sauce, white pepper, and magic powder (the quantity of leaves will seem much greater than the eggs, but that is fine).

Heat the oil in an 8-inch (20 cm) nonstick skillet over medium heat. Gently pour the omelet batter into the skillet. As the eggs begin to set, use a spatula to pull the edges of the omelet toward the center and let the eggs run underneath. Continue pulling until the bottom of the eggs are set but the surface is still runny, about 2 minutes.

Carefully flip the omelet in the pan, using a spatula like you would flip a pancake, and allow the top of the omelet to cook until both sides of the omelet are golden brown and the edges are crispy, another 1 to 2 minutes (or finish in the oven by baking the omelet at 325°F (165°C) until fully cooked, about 2 minutes).

Carefully slide the omelet from the skillet onto a clean cutting board and cut into small squares.

TO SERVE:

Place the omelet pieces onto a serving platter with the pan-fried mackerel, and serve with cha-om, nam prik grapi, steamed rice, cilantro, plus pork rinds, cucumber, cabbage, Thai chiles, Thai eggplant, turkey berry eggplant, and green beans for dipping.

Khao Kluk Grapi

Shrimp Paste Rice with Caramelized Pork and Accoutrements

Serves 4

Something we Thai people commonly brag about is how flavorful our food is, with an emphasis on sweet, sour, salty, and rich notes. So much of Thai food contains different permutations of these flavors, but one of my favorite ways to taste everything all at once is through khao kluk grapi, or shrimp paste rice with all its fixings. This dish is so colorful and fun because of its many components and how it is mixed at the table. The savory, shrimp paste–coated rice is piled in the center of a serving platter and then the accoutrements (like egg ribbons, sweet sticky pork, sharp slivers of green mango, raw shallots, Chinese sausage, and dried shrimp) are arranged around the rice like colorful numbers on a clock. I just love how when the platter is all tossed together, each bite of this can be a completely different experience depending on what you scoop up.

For the sausage:

2 links (3 ounces / 80 g) Chinese sausage, thinly sliced

For the egg ribbons:

2 large eggs

1 teaspoon fish sauce

1 teaspoon sugar

Pinch of ground white pepper

For the pork:

1 tablespoon neutral oil, such as sunflower

¼ cup (30 g) chopped white onion

1 teaspoon finely chopped garlic

1 teaspoon finely chopped, peeled fresh ginger

8 ounces (225 g) boneless pork shoulder, trimmed, thinly sliced, and cut into 1-inch (2.5 cm) squares

1½ tablespoons sugar

1 tablespoon fish sauce

1 tablespoon Thai seasoning sauce

2 tablespoons chopped preserved sweet radish

For the shrimp paste rice:

½ teaspoon shrimp paste

1 tablespoon fish sauce

1½ teaspoons sugar

1½ teaspoons Magic Powder (aka Asian chicken bouillon)

3 cups (570 g) day-old steamed rice

For the platter:

¼ cup (65 g) green mango or sour apple, cut into thin strips

¼ cup (20 g) dried shrimp

¼ cup (30 g) thinly sliced green beans

¼ cup (30 g) thinly sliced red onion

¼ cup (20 g) fresh cilantro leaves

1 teaspoon thinly sliced fresh Thai chile (optional)

4 lime cheeks (see page 50)

(Recipe continues)

MAKE THE SAUSAGE:

In a large skillet over medium heat, cook the sausage for 1 to 2 minutes, lightly tossing until the fat releases and the color of the sausage deepens from pink to red. Remove from the heat and set aside.

MAKE THE EGG RIBBONS:

In a medium bowl, scramble the eggs with the fish sauce, sugar, and white pepper.

Heat an 8-inch (20 cm) nonstick skillet over medium-high heat. Ladle a thin layer of the egg mixture onto the pan, like a crepe, until it is golden and set, about 2 minutes. Gently lift one side of the egg "crepe" using a rubber spatula and pinch the end with your fingers, then use your other hand to pinch along the other edge to lift slightly and flip. Cook for about another 30 seconds to set, then transfer to a cutting board to cool. Repeat with the remaining egg mixture. When cooled, stack the egg "crepes," roll them into a cylinder, and cut into ¼-inch-thick (6 mm) slices. Set aside.

MAKE THE PORK:

Heat the oil in a large skillet over medium-high heat. Add the onion, garlic, and ginger and cook until translucent and fragrant, about 1 minute. Add the pork and cook on one side, about 2 minutes. Using tongs, flip the pork and add the sugar, fish sauce, and Thai seasoning sauce. Cook, stirring, until the pork begins to caramelize and is cooked through, about 2 minutes. Add the sweet preserved radish and toss to combine. Transfer to a serving bowl and set aside.

MAKE THE SHRIMP PASTE RICE:

Using the same skillet (do not clean) over medium-high heat, add ¼ cup (60 ml) water with the shrimp paste, fish sauce, sugar, and magic powder and cook, stirring, until fragrant, about 1 minute. Once the paste mixture begins to bubble, add the rice and toss until everything is evenly combined. Transfer to the bowl with the pork and cover with a plate or lid to keep warm.

ASSEMBLE THE PLATTER:

Place a plate or large platter on top of the bowl with the pork and shrimp paste rice. Carefully flip the bowl and plate, holding the bowl onto the platter, so the plate lands on the work surface and the bowl is upside-down on top. Remove the bowl, creating a mound of rice in the center of the platter. In small piles around the perimeter of the rice mound, arrange the sausage, egg ribbons, green mango or sour apple, dried shrimp, green beans, red onion, cilantro leaves, and Thai chile, if using. Just before serving, squeeze the lime cheeks over the top. Using two spoons, toss everything together and serve.

Khanom Jeen

Curry Broth, Vermicelli Noodles, and Accoutrements

Serves 4

The magic of khanom jeen lies in the round, fermented vermicelli noodles, which act as a spectacular vehicle for the many curries of Thailand. Green curry, fish curry, and red cotton flower curry are all common pairings with these bouncy rice-based noodles, but I'm teaching you how to make my favorite, khanom jeen nam yah, a red curry–based stew paired with canned tuna and fish balls. This truly becomes a platter spectacular when you incorporate pickled mustard greens, Thai basil, and sliced cucumbers to cool off the palate. I love that for this dish the noodles and curries are prepared separately, so you can customize each bowl to be soupy or dry depending on your preference. The traditional fermented vermicelli noodles can be hard to find; so here I've opted for somen-style wheat noodles, which are just as effective. Have your condiment caddy within arm's reach to really make this dish pop.

For the khanom jeen curry:

- 2 krachai roots (40 g) or ½ bunch cilantro roots
- 1 (1-inch / 2.5 cm) piece peeled, fresh galangal, chopped
- 2 cloves garlic, peeled
- 2 tablespoon red curry paste
- 2 cups (480 ml) coconut milk
- 2 cups (480 ml) Nam Sai (Clear Bone Broth, page 178)
- 1 tablespoon fish sauce
- 2 (6-ounce / 170 g) cans solid white tuna in water, drained and flaked
- 1 (8-ounce / 225 g) package fish balls, defrosted
- 1 (15-ounce / 425 g) can hard-cooked quail eggs, drained

For serving:

- ¼ cup (20 g) shredded green cabbage
- ¼ cup (30 g) pickled mustard greens, thinly sliced
- ¼ cup (30 g) green beans, thinly sliced
- ¼ cup (25 g) thinly sliced shallots
- ¼ cup (10 g) fresh Thai basil leaves
- 8 ounces (225 g) somen-style wheat vermicelli noodles, cooked according to package instructions
- Lime cheeks (see page 50)
- Prik Nam Pla (Chile Fish Sauce, page 56)

MAKE THE KHANOM JEEN CURRY:

In a mortar with a pestle, pound together the krachai or cilantro stems, galangal, garlic, and red curry paste until a paste forms, about 10 minutes.

In a large saucepan, cook the curry paste with 2 tablespoons of the coconut milk over medium heat, stirring, until it's fragrant and deepens in color, about 2 minutes. Add the nam sai and fish sauce and simmer for 3 minutes. Add the tuna, fish balls, and quail eggs to the pot and simmer for another 3 minutes. Add the remaining coconut milk and simmer for 3 minutes to marry all the flavors.

TO SERVE:

Transfer the curry into a large serving bowl. Arrange the green cabbage, pickled mustard greens, green beans, shallots, and Thai basil around the curry bowl. Place a small noodle bundle into 4 small serving bowls and pour the curry over the noodles. Garnish as desired and serve with lime cheeks and prik nam pla.

Khao Mahn Gai

Chicken Fat Rice with KMG Sauce and Ginger Broth

Serves 4

Chicken fat rice is one of life's greatest comforts. You may know this dish as Hainanese chicken rice or Singaporean chicken rice, but in Thailand we call it khao mahn gai, or chicken fat rice. The name is apt because soft jasmine rice is steamed with chicken fat and broth—along with fragrant scallions, garlic, and ginger—for an enticingly flavorful base.

Traditionally, khao mahn gai is served with poached chicken, but fried chicken can be used as well, if you want to whip up a side of Hat Yai chicken (page 235)! Beyond the rice and chicken, sauce is what ties the dish together. There are sweet and dark soy sauces commonly found at the khao mahn gai stands across Thailand, but my favorite is the zesty soybean paste sauce. It's punchy with garlic and ginger, and a balance of vinegar and soy sauce. You're going to want to spoon it on everything. When I eat khao mahn gai, I take the fabulous sauce and drizzle a little over a bite of rice and spoon it into my mouth. Then I take a little chicken and dip it into the sauce and eat it. Then I take a sip of soup and a bite of cucumber and repeat it, over and over again.

For the khao mahn gai (KMG) sauce:

- 1/4 cup (60 ml) black soy sauce
- 2 tablespoons thin soy sauce
- 2 tablespoons vinegar from Pickled Garlic and Vinegar (page 62) or distilled vinegar
- 2 teaspoons sugar
- 2 tablespoons minced Pickled Garlic (page 62) or fresh garlic
- 2 tablespoons minced, peeled fresh ginger
- 6 fresh cilantro stems, thinly sliced
- 1/4 cup (60 ml) thao jiew (fermented soybean paste)
- 2 tablespoons chopped fresh cilantro leaves

For the ginger broth:

- 2 quarts (2 L) chicken broth
- 1 (1-inch / 2.5 cm) knob fresh ginger, peeled and cut into 1/8-inch (3 mm) slices on the bias
- 3 cloves garlic, smashed and peeled
- 1 tablespoon Magic Powder (aka Asian chicken bouillon)

For the rice and chicken:

- 3 cups (558 g) jasmine rice
- 2 skin-on, boneless chicken breasts (1½ pounds / 680 g), skin removed and chopped
- 2 skin-on, boneless chicken thighs (8 ounces / 170 g), skin removed and chopped
- 1 teaspoon toasted sesame oil
- Kosher salt
- 2 tablespoons neutral oil, such as sunflower
- 5 cloves garlic, chopped
- 1/4 cup (30 g) chopped white onion

For serving:

- Fresh cilantro springs
- Cucumber slices
- Sliced scallions

(Recipe continues)

MAKE THE KMG SAUCE:

In medium bowl, combine the black soy sauce, thin soy sauce, vinegar, sugar, pickled garlic, fresh garlic, ginger, cilantro stems, and ¼ cup (60 ml) water and whisk until the sugar dissolves, about 1 minute.

In a large bowl, combine the thao jiew and cilantro leaves. Stir in the soy-vinegar sauce to combine and set aside.

MAKE THE GINGER BROTH:

In a medium saucepan, heat the chicken broth, ginger, garlic, and magic powder over medium heat until warm.

MAKE THE RICE AND CHICKEN:

Using a fine-mesh sieve, rinse the rice until the water runs clear. Strain and set aside.

Coat the chicken with the sesame oil and a light sprinkle of salt. Let stand at room temperature for 30 minutes to marinate.

In a 5-quart (4.7 L) Dutch oven with a lid, combine the neutral oil and chicken skin. Cook the chicken skin over low heat until it's golden and crispy and the fat has rendered, about 6 minutes. Add the garlic and onion and cook until they are translucent, about 2 minutes. Add the rinsed rice and stir to coat the rice completely with the rendered chicken fat. Place the chicken onto the rice in an even layer. Pour half (1 quart / 960 ml) of the hot broth over the chicken and increase the heat to bring to a boil. Reduce the heat to maintain a simmer, cover, and simmer until the rice is tender but still al dente and the chicken is cooked through (when the internal temperature reads 165°F (74°C) on an instant-read thermometer), 15 to 20 minutes. (Keep in mind that the rice should be slightly al dente since less liquid is used than for a standard steamed rice recipe.)

Remove the chicken and transfer to a cutting board. Let cool slightly and cut into slices. Fluff the rice with a fork.

TO SERVE:

Place one-quarter of the rice into each of 4 serving bowls and top with slices of chicken breast and thigh and some cilantro sprigs. Serve the chicken and rice with a plate of cucumber and scallions alongside, the KMG sauce in a ramekin, and 4 small bowls filled with 1 cup (240 ml) garlic broth topped with scallions for sipping.

Hat Yai Fried Chicken

Southern Thai Fried Chicken with Dipping Sauces, Sticky Rice, and Cucumber Achaar

Serves 4

I was born and raised in Tennessee, so it seems inevitable that I fry chicken. I love that every culture has a version of fried chicken: sticky gochujang-coated chicken from Korea, bite-size karaage dunked in mayonnaise in Japan, and buttermilk-brined chicken in the States. This is my version of Thai fried chicken, named after the southern city in Thailand where this style hails from. There's Malaysian influence in this dish thanks to the blanket of fried shallots that finish the dish (similar to Malaysian-style chicken biryani). It's known for its light and airy crust, unctuous garlic and cilantro marinade, and that unforgettable crown of fried shallots. Pair this with sticky rice, sriracha, and spicy nam jim jaeow.

For the marinade (see Note for alternative ingredients):

- 6 cloves garlic, peeled
- 1 bunch fresh cilantro stems, leaves reserved for serving
- 1½ teaspoons sugar
- 1½ teaspoons kosher salt
- 1½ teaspoons ground white pepper
- ⅓ cup (75 ml) oyster sauce
- 1 tablespoon Thai seasoning sauce

For the chicken:

- 1 (5-pound / 2.3 kg) whole chicken (or 2 wings, 2 thighs, 2 drumsticks, and 2 breast pieces, split in half if large, skin on)
- Neutral oil, such as sunflower, for frying (about 8 cups / 2 L)
- 3 cups (315 g) rice flour
- 1½ cups (190 g) cornstarch
- Pinch of Chinese five-spice powder
- 2 cups (480 ml) soda water

For serving:

- Fried Shallots (page 64), or store-bought fried shallots
- Fresh cilantro sprigs
- Sriracha (page 60), or store-bought sriracha
- Nam Jim Jaeow (Dried Chile Sauce, page 72)
- Sticky Rice (page 38)
- Cucumber Achaar (page 196)

(Recipe continues)

MAKE THE MARINADE:

In a mortar with a pestle, grind the garlic and cilantro with the sugar, salt, and white pepper until a paste forms. Add the oyster sauce and seasoning sauce and stir to evenly combine (see Note).

MAKE THE CHICKEN:

Using kitchen shears or a knife, make a small slit where the leg meets the body and turn the leg out until it pops and exposes the bone. Slice through to remove the legs at the joint. Repeat on the other side. Slice each thigh from the drumstick. Then remove each breast by slicing, in long, smooth slices, along the centerbone, all the way through to remove the breast from the back. (Split the boneless breasts in half if they are too large and set aside.) Find where the wings connect to the body, and slice through the joint to remove. Store the carcass in a freezer-safe container in the freezer for up to 3 months for future recipes, like broth (see page 178).

Place the chicken pieces in a large zip-top freezer bag, cover with the marinade, and shake so the chicken is evenly coated. For the best results, marinate the chicken in the refrigerator for 24 hours, or at least 12 hours.

Pour oil to come 1½ inches (4 cm) up the sides of a large, deep stockpot or Dutch oven. Heat over medium heat to 325°F (165°C) when measured with a deep-fry thermometer.

In a high-sided baking dish, combine the rice flour, cornstarch, and five-spice powder. Dip the marinated chicken in the rice flour–cornstarch mixture until fully coated on each side. Dust off the excess dredge. Working in batches, use a spider or slotted spoon to carefully place the dredged chicken into the hot oil, leaving room in the pot so the chicken can dance around. Par-fry, flipping halfway through, for 6 minutes. Remove the chicken and rest on a wire rack for about 5 minutes. Bring the oil back up to temperature and repeat with the remaining chicken.

Gradually whisk the soda water into the dish with the remaining dredge until the consistency is similar to milk.

Lightly coat the rested chicken pieces with the wet dredge and return them to the oil. Fry, flipping halfway through, until the chicken reaches an internal temperature of 325°F (165°C) when measured with a deep-fry thermometer, about 6 minutes.

TO SERVE:

Serve immediately, garnished with a generous portion of fried shallots, cilantro leaves, and sides of sriracha, nam jim jaeow, sticky rice, and cucumber achaar.

Note: If you don't have a mortar and pestle, you can make a slightly different version of the marinade, which involves a little more chopping, using the following ingredients:

1 tablespoon chopped garlic

¼ cup (20 g) chopped fresh cilantro stems

⅓ cup (75 ml) oyster sauce

1 tablespoon Thai seasoning sauce

1½ teaspoons kosher salt

1½ teaspoons sugar

1½ teaspoons ground white pepper

SRIRACHA
Chili

AROY-D
PALM'S SEED
(ATTAP) IN HEAVY SYRUP
SARABHA'S CREAMERY
EST. 2022
POCKY
CHOCOLATE
CHOCOLATE CREAM COVERED BISCUIT STICKS
NET WT. 2.47oz (70g)
POCKY
STRAWBERRY
STRAWBERRY CREAM COVERED BISCUIT STICKS
NET WT. 2.47oz (70g)

The word for *dessert* in Thai is the same word used for the word *snack: khanom*. I love the concept of khanom being both an after-dinner sweet and something to indulge in in the middle of the day. One of the reasons khanom functions as a snack so well is because Thai desserts frequently border on savory, thanks to salted coconut cream, corn, and so many other unique ingredients. I won't judge if you prepare any of these recipes for breakfast—or as an afternoon snack. What I will say is that this chapter will show you how varied Thai desserts can be—silky and custardy, chilled and refreshing, textured and salty, warm and comforting. We're not just crafting mango sticky rice here; we'll get more inventive with a fancy fruit and sticky rice plate (page 242), fried cookies shaped like flowers (page 248), and a classic Thai ice cream sandwich that uses actual bread as a base (page 258). There is a Thai dessert for every palate, and I'm going to show you how easy and visually striking these sweets can be.

Cream of the Crop

On my last trip to Thailand, I went to a homestay bed and breakfast in Bang Yai of the Nonthaburi province, an area just outside of the metropolis that is Bangkok. The traditional Thai teak and apexed roofed accommodation was beautifully designed and surrounded by a serene, picturesque landscape. The purpose of this trip was to experience as much Thai food as possible, but I did have my hesitations when my guide booked me into a cooking class there. The last thing I wanted was a watered-down, touristy cooking class.

To my delight, they offered a nuanced introduction to many of the fundamentals of Thai cuisine. We made a curry from scratch, pounding out the curry paste from ingredients that were procured from the market earlier that morning. The icing on the cake was when it came time to work with coconut milk—one of the gardeners at the B&B climbed a coconut tree, cut down a few fresh coconuts, and handed them over to us to make our own coconut water, cream, and milk. I had never cooked with coconut milk that didn't come from a can! I marveled at the process of extracting coconut milk and wanted to share my findings from that day with you here.

The coconut has four edible components: flesh, coconut water, coconut cream, and coconut milk. But it takes a bit of work to get them. First, we cracked the shell in half (and by we, I mean the gardener, who chopped the coconut open using a machete he wielded almost *too* comfortably). The coconut released a thin, almost clear liquid, the coconut water that so many of us love to drink.

Then, after scraping a few shards of flesh to snack on, we grated the rest of the coconut on a grathai, or rabbit, a tool that gets its name due to its rudimentary resemblance of a bunny with a carrot in its mouth. Because being seated makes it easier to put your muscle into the grating, there's a bench with a jagged blade where the rabbit's mouth can rest. Beneath the rabbit, we laid a tray to catch all the grated coconut, falling like snowflakes from the rabbit's jagged mouth. After the coconut shell was empty of the meat, it came time to make the coconut milk. Squeezing the grated flesh extracted a thick, white liquid with a strong coconut flavor, known as the coconut cream. It's great for finishing desserts and savory recipes, almost like how heavy cream is used in French cooking.

Next, the grated coconut is rinsed with the coconut water that came out at the start of the process and then squeezed, releasing a second round of liquid, what we know to be coconut milk. How cool is that?!

Coconut is one of the most popular flavors in Thailand, for smoothies, layer cakes, and ice creams. In this cookbook, you'll put coconut to use many times, when making sweets, like ruam mitt (page 246), as well as in curries and soup. The leftover grated coconut can be toasted and added to so many sweets and savory dishes, too.

It's amazing that so many ingredients can come out of a singular fruit—all of which are integral to Thai cooking. To me, this entire coconut lesson was a reminder that the world of food is a limitless opportunity for growth and knowledge. I hope that this cookbook serves as a similar opportunity for learning and is equally exciting to you as seeing fresh coconut milk produced was to me!

Fancy Fruit Sticky Rice

Fruit Tart Meets Mango Sticky Rice

Serves 4

I know that everyone loves a classic mango sticky rice—trust me, I do, too. But I wanted to make a dessert that celebrates fruits of all seasons. I think of my fancy fruit and sticky rice as a fruit tart that had a baby with mango sticky rice. There's still the lush, coconut milk–drenched sticky rice you know and love, with the kiss of pandan, but I've incorporated more fruit so the mango doesn't always have to do the heavy lifting. I've made this with kiwi, dragonfruit, lychee, blueberry, pineapple, and pomelo, but you can play around with any of your favorite fruits or adapt the recipe based on the season. To really set this dessert off, I often top it with a scoop of coconut sorbet.

For the coconut "icing":

- 1 tablespoon rice flour
- 1 cup (240 ml) coconut milk
- Pinch of kosher salt

For the pandan sticky rice:

- 1 cup (240 ml) coconut milk
- ¾ cup (170 g) sugar
- ½ teaspoon pandan extract
- 1 teaspoon kosher salt
- 12 ounces (340 g) cooked sticky rice (about 2 cups; see page 38)

For serving:

- Seasonal fruit, thinly sliced
- Toasted mung beans (see Note)
- Basil seed syrup (see Note, page 246)

MAKE THE COCONUT "ICING":

In a small saucepan, combine the rice flour and 1 tablespoon water, place over medium heat, and whisk until smooth. Add the coconut milk and salt and whisk until slightly thickened, about 4 minutes. Remove from the heat and let cool to room temperature. (You can serve it at room temperature or chilled. It will thicken more as it cools.)

MAKE THE PANDAN STICKY RICE:

In a medium saucepan, combine the coconut milk, sugar, pandan extract, and salt. Place over medium-low heat, bring to a simmer, and simmer, stirring, until the sugar is completely dissolved, about 3 minutes. Remove from the heat. Drizzle a little of the coconut milk mixture over the rice and fold it in until it's absorbed, adding more sauce as needed, until the rice is well coated and slightly creamy but not too wet.

TO SERVE:

Divide the pandan rice among 4 bowls (or make it fancy by filling a 4-inch cookie cutter or ring mold with the pandan rice to create a disk of rice on each plate to decorate with fruit and garnishes) and top each bowl with sliced seasonal fruit, toasted mung beans, and dollops of the coconut icing and basil seed syrup.

Note:

To make the toasted mung beans:

Place ¼ cup (45 g) dried yellow mung beans in a fine-mesh sieve and rinse them until the water runs clear to remove any debris. Set aside.

In a small saucepan, bring 1 cup (240 ml) water to a boil over high heat. Stir in the beans, reduce the heat to maintain a simmer, and cook until almost tender, about 15 minutes.

Drain well and transfer to a medium, dry nonstick skillet. Place over medium heat and cook, tossing, until crisp and golden brown, about 12 minutes. Set aside.

Tap Tim Krob

Ruby Chestnuts in Coconut Soup

Serves 4

As a kid, my favorite part of ruam mitt (see page 246) were these almost boba-like ruby-hued water chestnuts (opposite). I would always make it a priority to scoop these out from the mix of other sweet delights first. But it wasn't until I was twelve visiting Chatuchak (Bangkok's largest outdoor market) that I discovered a vendor selling tap tim krob, a bowl strictly consisting of these gems, a total game changer.

For the coconut soup:

- 2 cups (480 ml) coconut milk
- 1 cup (200 g) sugar
- 1 pandan leaf or ½ teaspoon pandan extract (or vanilla extract)
- Pinch of kosher salt

For the jasmine syrup:

- ½ cup (110 g) sugar
- ½ teaspoon jasmine flavor extract

For the ruby chestnuts:

- 1 (8-ounce / 225 g) can diced water chestnuts, drained
- ½ teaspoon red food coloring
- 1 cup (130 g) tapioca starch

For serving:

- Shaved ice or ice cubes

MAKE THE COCONUT SOUP:

In a medium saucepan, combine the coconut milk, sugar, pandan, and salt. Bring to a simmer over medium-low heat and simmer, stirring occasionally, until the sugar is dissolved, about 2 minutes. Cover and refrigerate until ready to serve (if you used a pandan leaf, remove it after 1 hour). You will have 2½ cups (600 ml).

MAKE THE JASMINE SYRUP:

In a medium saucepan, combine the sugar, ½ cup (120 ml) water, and the jasmine extract. Place over medium heat and bring to a simmer. Once the sugar has dissolved, about 2 minutes, let the liquid cool and set aside. You will have ½ cup (120 ml) syrup.

MAKE THE RUBY CHESTNUTS:

Fill a large saucepan three-quarters full of water and bring to a boil over high heat. Make an ice bath by filling a large bowl with ice and cold water.

In a medium bowl, using a spoon, toss the water chestnuts with the red food coloring and 2 tablespoons water until the water chestnuts become vibrant red. You will have 1½ cups (360 g) water chestnuts.

Put the tapioca starch in a separate large bowl. Dredge the red water chestnuts in the tapioca starch until they are fully coated. Transfer to a mesh strainer to shake off any excess starch **(1)**. Set aside.

Using a spider or slotted spoon and working in batches, gently lower the water chestnuts into the water. Cook until the tapioca starch begins to turn translucent and the water chestnuts float, about 2 minutes **(2)**. Remove from the boiling water and transfer to the ice bath **(3)**. Repeat with remaining water chestnuts. Once cooled, transfer the cooked water chestnuts into the jasmine syrup **(4)**.

TO SERVE:

Place some shaved ice into 4 serving bowls. Ladle the water chestnut "ruby pearls" over the ice in each bowl and top with the syrup. Give the coconut soup a quick whisk and pour it evenly among the bowls over the ruby pearls and serve immediately. Store any remaining coconut soup and ruby chestnuts in syrup in separate airtight containers in the refrigerator for up to 3 days.

1

2

3

4

Khanom Ruam Mitt
Chilled Fruit Cocktail in Coconut Soup

Serves 8

The word *ruam* means "together," and this customizable dish assembles a bunch of fun components: jewel-toned water chestnuts coated in a sticky cornstarch batter, bright yellow slices of jackfruit, and colorful jellies and fruits. You can make it your own by adding or omitting whatever sweets you like. It's essentially a Thai fruit cocktail enhanced with refreshing coconut milk. And when packed in to-go plastic bags with floating ice cubes, it really feels like something you'd get from a Thai vendor.

For the soup:

- 4 cups (960 ml) coconut milk
- 1 cup (200 g) sugar
- 1 teaspoon salt

Some ideas for the fruit salad:

- Tap Tim Krob (page 244)
- Assorted canned jellies from an Asian market, such as grass, pandan, and almond jelly
- Canned whole lychee in syrup
- Canned palm seeds in syrup
- Canned longan berry in syrup
- Canned jackfruit in syrup
- Jarred red mung beans in syrup
- Red grapes, halved
- Golden mango, cut into ½-inch pieces
- Candied gingko nuts (see Notes)
- Basil seed syrup (see Notes)
- Assorted edible flower petals

MAKE THE SOUP:

In a large saucepan, bring 1 cup (240 ml) of the coconut milk to a simmer over medium heat. Add the sugar and salt and whisk until fully dissolved, about 3 minutes. Remove from the heat and whisk in the remaining 3 cups (720 ml) coconut milk. Transfer to a serving bowl, cover, and let cool in the refrigerator until ready to serve, at least 30 minutes. You will have 4½ cups (1 liter) soup.

MAKE THE FRUIT SALAD:

Transfer all the jellies and fruits from the cans and jars into separate bowls or ramekins to build a toppings station for serving, like an ice cream sundae bar.

TO SERVE:

Build your own fruit cocktail by placing fruits and jellies into your bowl. Quickly whisk the coconut soup, in case it separated, and pour it over the fruits and jellies in each bowl. Garnish with the basil seed syrup and edible flower petals. Store any remaining coconut soup in an airtight container in the refrigerator for up to 4 days.

Notes: Gingko nuts are found at Asian markets in the refrigerator section already shelled in vacuum-sealed parcels. In their raw state, they tend to be very bitter. To prepare: Split the nuts in half and remove the tiny center bitter seed. In a medium saucepan, simmer the gingko nuts in a 1-part sugar and 1-part water simple syrup mixture over low heat until tender but not mushy and infused with the syrup, 20 to 25 minutes. Let cool in the liquid. Store in an airtight container in the refrigerator for up to 1 month.

I love using basil seeds for an extra flourish. To prepare: Make a simple syrup with 1 cup (240 ml) water, 1 cup (200 g) sugar, and 3 cardamom pods; heat over medium heat, stirring, to dissolve the sugar, 2 to 3 minutes. While the syrup is hot, strain the liquid through a fine-mesh sieve over ¼ cup (40 g) basil seeds and let the seeds rehydrate for at least 30 minutes before using. Store in an airtight container in the refrigerator for up to 1 month. If they get gummy, add a splash of water to loosen.

Khanom Dhok Jhok
Crispy Lotus Blossom Tuiles

Makes 26 cookies

Flowers are such an influential part of Thai sweets, both for their aesthetics and their flavors. You can find syrupy jasmine sweets all around Thailand. Although these dhok jhok cookies aren't flavored with floral notes, they're incredibly beautiful, like a lotus in bloom. Sesame adds a pleasantly nutty flavor to these crisp cookies. They may seem intimidating to make, but I promise you they're relatively simple! Just prep the batter and get ready to fry. You do need a special iron to make them—they are similar to Mexican rosettes—but once you have one, easily ordered online, be prepared to wow your friends with these fragrant, sesame-studded bites.

For the limestone water:

1 teaspoon red limestone paste

For the batter:

¼ cup (35 g) all-purpose flour

½ cup (55 g) rice flour

⅓ cup (46 g) tapioca starch

¼ cup (55 g) sugar

½ teaspoon kosher salt

½ cup (120 ml) coconut milk

1 large egg

¼ cup (60 ml) limestone water

1½ teaspoons neutral oil, such as sunflower, plus additional for frying

1 tablespoon black sesame seeds

Lavender or jasmine honey, for serving

Black and white sesame seeds, for serving

MAKE THE LIMESTONE WATER:

In a lidded glass container, add the limestone paste and 2 cups (480 ml) water; cover and shake vigorously to combine. The stone particles will break down and float around but will not dissolve. Once the stones settle to the bottom and the liquid is clear, at least 6 hours, use the water on the top and leave the stones at the bottom.

MAKE THE BATTER:

In a large bowl, combine the all-purpose flour, rice flour, tapioca starch, sugar, and salt. Add the coconut milk, egg, and ¼ cup (60 ml) limestone water and whisk everything together until smooth. Slowly whisk in the oil. Set a fine-mesh sieve on top of a separate bowl and strain the batter through it. Stir in the sesame seeds and set aside.

FINISH THE COOKIES:

Pour enough oil to come 2 inches (5 cm) up the sides of a large saucepan. Heat over medium heat to 325°F (165C) when measured with a deep-fry thermometer.

Prime the cookie mold by placing it into the hot oil for 10 seconds. Let excess oil drip from the mold before dipping the stamp straight into the batter, just to its rim, without submerging it completely (or it will not release in the oil). Quickly lower the stamp under the surface of the hot oil and jiggle the mold until the cookie releases into the oil. Fry the cookie, flipping once, until both sides are golden, 2 to 3 minutes. Remove from the oil and transfer to a paper towel–lined plate to drain excess oil. Maintain the 325°F (165C) oil temperature while frying the remaining batter, making sure the mold is free of any cookie remnants before dipping into the batter. Serve at room temperature with a drizzle of honey and a sprinkle of sesame seeds. Or store in an airtight container for up to 1 week.

Thah Ko
Corn and Tapioca Pudding

Serves 6

If you haven't noticed yet, Thai desserts are all about layers. Thah ko is a layered pudding that features pops of sweet corn swimming in a tapioca base. It's typically crowned with a luscious and slightly salty coconut cream topping that makes for a perfect balance of sweet, savory, and fragrant. Traditionally, thah ko would be served in kratongs, or mini baskets crafted from pandan or banana leaves, which lend an earthy note to the dish. Although that presentation is old-school and fun, trust me when I tell you it's just as good in mini ceramic or glass bowls.

For the pudding:

- 2 medium ears corn, husks and silks removed
- ½ cup (85 g) small tapioca pearls
- 2 cups (480 ml) coconut milk
- ½ cup (100 g) sugar
- ½ teaspoon pandan extract
- Pinch of kosher salt
- Edible flower petals, for serving

For the coconut topping:

- 2 tablespoons unsweetened shredded coconut
- 1 tablespoon sugar
- ½ teaspoon salt

For the cream:

- 1 cup (240 ml) coconut cream
- Pinch of kosher salt
- 2 tablespoons cornstarch

MAKE THE PUDDING:

Using a knife, slice the end of the corn cob off to create a flat surface. Holding the cob vertically (with the flat end on the cutting board or a baking sheet), carefully shave the raw kernels from each cob. Set aside.

Place the tapioca pearls in a fine-mesh sieve and gently rinse them for 15 seconds to remove any excess starch. Set aside.

In a large saucepan, bring 1½ cups (360 ml) water to a boil over high heat. Reduce the heat to medium. Add the rinsed tapioca pearls and cook, stirring constantly, until the tapioca thickens and becomes translucent, 10 to 12 minutes. Stir in the coconut milk, sugar, pandan extract, and salt, bring to a simmer, and simmer, stirring, for 3 more minutes. Fold in half of the corn kernels and remove from the heat.

Divide the pudding among 6 individual ceramic or glass cups and let stand for 10 minutes.

MAKE THE COCONUT TOPPING:

In a small bowl, combine the remaining half of the corn kernels with the coconut, sugar, and salt. Set aside.

MAKE THE CREAM:

In a small saucepan, combine the coconut milk and salt and bring to a simmer over medium heat.

Meanwhile, make a cornstarch slurry: In a small bowl, combine the cornstarch with 2 tablespoons water and whisk until the cornstarch is fully dissolved.

Whisk the slurry into the coconut milk until it thickens, about 2 minutes. Remove from the heat. Spoon a thin layer of the cream onto each tapioca pudding, sprinkle with the coconut topping, garnish with edible flower petals, and serve immediately. Cover any remaining custards and refrigerate for up to 3 days.

Kluay Buat Chee
Poached Bananas

Serves 4

The two words I'd use to describe this sweet treat are quick and easy. In its simplest form, bananas are poached in a sweetened coconut syrup. You can stop there—the bananas in the coconut broth are elegant as is—but I love to spruce it up with mini pretzels for added crunch and thinly sliced makrut lime leaves for color and aroma. The best part is that this dish barely takes any work and also happens to be vegan.

- 1½ cups (360 ml) coconut cream
- ½ cup (120 ml) almond milk
- ¼ cup (100 g) granulated sugar
- 1 (2-ounce / 55 g) disk palm sugar
- ¼ teaspoon almond extract
- 4 medium-ripe (yellow but not speckled) bananas, peeled

For serving:

- Mini pretzel twists, broken into large pieces
- Thinly sliced fresh makrut lime leaves, ribs removed

In a medium saucepan, combine the coconut milk, almond milk, granulated sugar, palm sugar, and almond extract and heat over medium heat, stirring until dissolved, about 5 minutes. Remove from the heat.

Add the bananas to the sauce and let stand at least 1 hour, occasionally flipping to coat in sauce, if needed, or cover and refrigerate up to 24 hours.

Reheat the bananas in the sauce over low heat until warmed through, about 5 minutes.

TO SERVE:

Transfer the bananas to a cutting board and slice on the bias into 2-inch (5 cm) pieces. Divide the pieces between 4 serving bowls and pour the sauce evenly over the top. Garnish with the pretzels and lime leaves.

Sangkaya Bai Toey
Pandan Egg Yolk Pudding with Toast

Serves 4 to 6

The leaves from the tropical screwpine plant are a cornerstone of Thai cooking in mostly sweet and some savory applications. Pandan possesses the most exquisite scent and delicate, floral flavor and has infiltrated practically every dessert in Thailand. You can find it in ice cream, crepe cakes, jellies, and more. One of the most classic iterations is pandan pudding, called sangkaya (like the kaya toast you find in Malaysia and Singapore), which is traditionally paired with steamed rolls. This is a common breakfast food or afterschool snack for many Thais. The combination of warm, fragrant custard with pillowy buns is hard to beat—you'll find yourself scraping the bottom of the bowl to get every last drop. Although traditionalists will source fresh pandan for their desserts, it is more difficult to find stateside. If you can get your hands on fresh pandan leaves, I encourage you to try processing them into juice. Otherwise, pandan extract works great and can be found in the baking section of most Asian grocery stores.

- 2 cups (480 ml) coconut milk
- 2 tablespoons cornstarch
- 1 cup (200 g) sugar
- ¼ teaspoon kosher salt
- 4 large egg yolks
- ½ teaspoon pandan extract

For serving:

- 4 to 6 slices thick-sliced white bread, like Texas Toast, or 2 to 3 Hawaiian rolls, toasted

Pour water into a medium saucepan to come 2 inches (5 cm) up the sides. Place over medium heat and bring to a simmer. (Alternatively, you can use a double boiler.)

In a separate medium saucepan, combine the coconut milk, cornstarch, sugar, and salt. Place over medium-low heat and cook, whisking, until the sugar is completely dissolved, about 1 minute. Remove from the heat.

Transfer the mixture into a metal bowl and whisk the egg yolks into the warm coconut milk mixture.

Reduce the heat under the water to keep it at a rolling simmer but not boiling. Place the bowl with the custard above the simmering water, making sure the water does not touch the bowl, and cook, whisking continuously, for about 10 minutes. (Do not rush this process or step away, to keep the eggs from scrambling.) Once the custard has thickened to a pudding-like consistency, remove the pan from the heat and pour it into ramekins or small serving bowls.

TO SERVE:

Serve the custard warm with toast or cover and refrigerate for up to 3 days. It can then be served chilled or brought to room temperature.

แฟนต้า

Sangkaya Fak Tong
Mom's Steamed Egg Custard in Pumpkins

Makes 6 custards

Every fall, while some families used pumpkins as decor, my family actually served dessert in them. Pumpkin custard, or sangkaya fak tong in Thai, is a lusciously smooth custard commonly enjoyed for breakfast or as a snack. My mom always prepared it for Thanksgiving. The pumpkin is steamed so that a knife can easily glide through the entire thing, making it easy to cut into wedges and serve individual slices. The custard mixture is fragrant and luxuriously smooth, the ideal foil to the crunch of granola.

6 mini pumpkins, seeded and cleaned (about 4 pounds / 1.8 kg)

For the custard:

- 1 cup (240 ml) coconut milk
- 1 teaspoon vanilla extract
- 1½ (2-ounce / 55 g) disks palm sugar or ½ cup (95 g) raw cane sugar
- ½ cup (100 g) granulated sugar
- Pinch of kosher salt
- Pinch of ground nutmeg
- Pinch of ground cinnamon
- 5 large eggs

For serving:

- Whipped cream
- Honey
- Granola
- Dulce de leche ice cream (optional)

MAKE THE CUSTARD:

Using a knife, carefully cut open the top of the pumpkin, around the stem, like you would when carving a jack-o'-lantern. Remove the top and set aside. With a spoon, scrape out all the seeds and stringy innards until the interior of the pumpkin is clean and discard (or save the seeds to roast later for snacks). Repeat with the remaining pumpkins and set aside.

Pour water into a saucepan large enough to fit a steamer basket to come 1 inch (2.5 cm) up the sides. Place over high heat and bring to a boil.

In a medium saucepan, combine the coconut milk, vanilla, palm sugar, granulated sugar, salt, nutmeg, and cinnamon. Place over medium-low heat and cook, stirring, until the sugar dissolves, about 2 minutes. Remove from the heat and let cool. Whisk in the eggs until completely incorporated. You should have about 2½ cups (600 ml). Pour the custard mixture evenly (a little less than ½ cup / 120 ml in each) into the pumpkins and top with the pumpkin stems. Transfer to the steamer basket.

Place the steamer basket over the pot with the boiling water. Cover and steam until the custard feels firm to the touch and the pumpkin can be easily pierced with the tip of a knife, 35 to 45 minutes.

TO SERVE:

Top each steamed pumpkin custard with a dollop of whipped cream, a drizzle of honey, and a spoonful of granola (and even a scoop of ice cream, if desired). Place the stem gently back on top, like a lid, and serve immediately.

Khanom Pang Ai Thiim
Ice Cream Sandwich on a Bun

Serves 4 to 8

I have so many memories associated with this style of ice cream sandwich. Every time I spotted the neon green and blue tarp caverns that make up the night markets of Bangkok, I knew ice cream vendors would be close by. This is the best type of ice cream sandwich (I don't even want to talk about those crumbly chocolate wafer versions). Thais love to use actual bread for their ice cream sandwiches—sometimes hot dog buns, sometimes brioche. Any soft white bread can fly here. The reason bread is such an excellent vessel for Thai sundaes is that it can hold a lot of toppings and soak up the delicious coconut ice cream. This ice cream sandwich has so much playful texture: sticky rice, roasted peanuts, strands of jackfruit, and drizzles of sweetened condensed milk are all common. You can completely customize the toppings to your preference, and if you really wanted to include some American classics like sprinkles, chocolate sauce, and cherries, that would work beautifully here, too.

For the sugar corn:

- 1 medium ear corn, husks and silks removed
- 2 tablespoons sugar
- Pinch of kosher salt

For the coconut:

- ¼ cup (20 g) sweet shredded coconut

For the ice cream sandwich:

- 8 sweet Hawaiian rolls or 4 hot dog buns
- 2 cups (590 g) pandan sticky rice (page 242)
- 1 pint (480 ml) coconut ice cream
- Sweetened condensed milk, to taste
- ½ cup (80 g) roasted, unsalted peanuts, roughly chopped
- Caramel corn (store-bought)

MAKE THE SUGAR CORN:

Using a knife, slice the end of the corn cob off to create a flat surface. Holding the cob vertically (with the flat end on the cutting board or baking sheet), carefully shave the raw kernels from the cob. In a medium bowl, toss the kernels with the sugar and salt. Set aside.

TOAST THE COCONUT:

In a dry medium skillet, toast the coconut over medium heat, stirring, until pale golden brown, 2 to 3 minutes. Transfer to a bowl and set aside.

ASSEMBLE THE SANDWICH:

Top your choice of roll or bun with a thin layer of the sweet sticky rice, followed by a scoop or two of ice cream. Drizzle the sweetened condensed milk over the ice cream and top with the sugar corn, peanuts, and caramel corn. Serve immediately.

Boozy Thai Coffee Affogato

Serves 4

You may notice I have a flair for what I'm calling Thai-Talian cuisine—Italian dishes with Thai sensibilities. Thai-Talian also extends to dessert. I've noticed at the restaurant that people love espresso martinis at any time of a day. They're great at lunch, at dinner, as an aperitif, or as a digestif. To satisfy my customers' craving for these boozy—and highly caffeinated—cocktails, I make a Thai coffee take. Thai black coffee, called *oliang*, is marked by a very deep, bitter flavor and ample sweetness thanks to scoops of brown sugar. I use an instant coffee drink called Cofe O-Lieng, but if you can't find it, I've also shared ways to prepare Thai coffee and syrup from scratch. If you *can* get your hands on the instant Cofe O-Lieng brand, proceed directly to the boozy Thai coffee portion of the recipe and ignore the syrup and Thai coffee instructions. To make this dish even more rich, I decided to add ice cream. You can use coffee ice cream, vanilla ice cream, or coconut ice cream—just swap out the espresso garnish for a star anise for an extra Thai touch.

For the syrup:

3 cardamom pods

½ cup (200 g) sugar

1 teaspoon sesame seeds

For the Thai coffee:

3 tablespoons instant coffee, such as Nescafé

2 tablespoons sugar

¼ cup (60 ml) hot water

½ cup (120 ml) cold water

For the affogato:

3 ounces (90 ml) vodka

3 ounces (90 ml) evaporated milk

1 pint (480 ml) vanilla ice cream

Espresso powder, for serving

MAKE THE CARDAMOM SYRUP:

In a medium saucepan, combine the cardamom pods with the sugar, sesame seeds, and ½ cup (120 ml) water. Bring to a simmer over medium-low heat and simmer until the sugar dissolves and reduces by one-third, about 8 minutes. Remove from the heat and let cool to room temperature. Strain through a fine-mesh sieve into an airtight container and store in the refrigerator for up to 2 weeks. This will make about ½ cup (120 ml).

MAKE THE THAI COFFEE:

In a lidded glass jar or other container with a lid, combine the instant coffee, sugar, and hot water and stir until completely dissolved. Pour in the cold water, cover, and refrigerate until ready to use. This will make about ¾ cup (180 ml).

MAKE THE BOOZY THAI COFFEE:

In a cocktail shaker, combine the vodka, evaporated milk, 1 ounce (30 ml) of the cardamom syrup, and the Thai iced coffee. Carefully fill the shaker with ice, cover, and shake vigorously.

TO SERVE:

Place a ½ cup (4-ounce / 115 g) scoop ice cream into each of 4 coupe glasses. Divide the coffee syrup mixture evenly among the coupes, over the ice cream. Dust each with espresso powder and serve immediately.

My International Market Story:
By Amanda Drooker

Some of my fondest memories of my early 20's took place @ International market! After a day of retail work at the mall, I would go to International market (at least once a week) and get an order of the India noodle with tofu. I loved Patti so much, and would watch top chef with her, or the news, or really whatever was on the TV at that moment!

Patti lives on at the New IM, and my heart is so full.

♡ Amanda ☺

My International Market Story:
By: EMMA

I had many an amazing lunch @ the old IM during my days at Belmont

friends ♡

My International Market Story:
By: Abram & Amanda

The Food at the I.M. is the First solid Food I ate as a baby. My parents Started coming here the week they opened in 75'-76'? I remember eating at low tables on the ground with cushions in the 80's. My mom's Friends lived in the house next door and we would hang out in the abandoned house behind the restaurant. I started bringing my wife here when we were First dating. She loved it immediately & we kept coming until they tore it down. We even got to buy some memorabilia from Patti. We love the I.M. and will always come back.

My International Market Story:
By: Katie Gillon

We've been coming to IM since we moved to the neighborhood in 1973. All 3 of my kids grew up eating here their entire lives. We loved Patti. She was the sweetest lady and would Always come over to talk to us and find out how everyone was doing. We remember little Amoed hanging out at the restaurant after school. We are so happy that IM is back and is so great. ♡

My International Market Story:

By: Amy Bergesen

Once I was taking a cooking class at PM with Arnold, + I was sitting next to Patti, Arnold's mom. Arnold was chatting while food sizzled, unattended, in a skillet. It seemed to sizzle for a long time. Patti and I both couldn't stop staring at the skillet. I whispered to her, "I really want to stir that." She whispered back, "Me too." We were always friendly after that. :)

My International Market story:

By: Isabella Kearney

Patti taught me to use chop sticks when I was 4 years old and she never gave me a fork ever again. I ended up stabbing ALOT of chicken with a chopstick when I was young. As I got older I continued to use chopsticks and now can eat anything just like Patti taught me.

Once I brought a date to IM and when he asked for a fork Patti and her sister look at me like "Are you sure you want to date this man?" So they gave him chopsticks and said "She'll teach you" :)

My International Market Story:

By Vivek Surti

Having Patti have a group of us sit around a table as she brought out her famous "House Salad"— I had never tried anything like it. True to what she said, it was a "flava explosion" and to this day, one of my favorite food memories.

STEAM TABLE
LUNCH 11-2
A LA CARTE 4
PICK THREE 11
@IMNASHVILLE
Fanta

- ACKNOWLEDGMENTS -

ARNOLD: This book has been fifty years in the making. Thanks to every person who has ever grabbed a red tray and shuffled down the cafeteria line at International Market. Thanks to the aunties in the kitchen, the students who worked summer jobs, and the generations of families that grew up with me. Thank you to the Nashville food community and journalists who, at a young age, planted my seed of culinary curiosity. Thanks to my sister, Anna, for getting me back in a Thai kitchen. Thanks to the new crop of chefs who inspire and push me to cook hard, with pride and integrity. Of course, shout out to my kid, Henley, for getting me to "adult" and focus on grounding our future. And most of all, thank you to the my parents for their vision and for a life well lived.

I like to say that it's not hard to make good food when you have good ingredients. The same sentiment goes for the heart of this book. Without the talents and support of my team, this book would still be a pipe dream.

Cheers to Kat Thompson; I could not have asked for a better Thai and English writing partner for this masterpiece.

To the entire creative team: Stan Okumura, Eric Howard, Jon Joiner, Courtney Knapp, Kate Knapp, Katy Stark, Linda Xiao, Judy Haubert, Ariagna Abreu, Magdalena Boujenah, Julie Choi, Diane Shaw, Laura Dozier, Jon Michael Darga, and my International Market family: Rhys Kay, Mac McCloskey, Riley Holingsworth, Ash Wilson, Kan Varapimrut, Aunt Mel, P. Kanjana Henderson, Aubrey Robinson, Pa Tongdee, and Pa Kong, we did it!!!

And to quote my mom, "Be good, I love you."

I also want to extend my gratitude to the Tourism Authority of Thailand, the Thai Royal Ministry of Commerce, Department of International Trade Promotions, Buchwald Agency, Aevitas Creative, Direct Message, Food Sheriff, Le Creuset, Friendly Arctic, Katie Haas, Bangkok Market, Pandan Market, Lauren Webb, Leo Kopsombut, Jose Munoz, and my Thai food community from coast to coast for being an integral and inspired part of this book. Thank you.

KAT: Thank you first and foremost to Arnold for entrusting me with your story and being the most collaborative and creative partner to work with.

Thank you to our editor, Laura Dozier, for her guiding hand and the entire creative team who touched this. I especially want to thank Courtney Knapp; we would not have been able to write this book without you.

To my closest friends who have seen me through so many highs and lows, I love you all (you know who you are). Thank you for never failing to make me laugh or put a smile on my face, and for the many sessions of potato-ing on couches or playing games together.

Endless appreciation for my family, who have been my biggest cheerleaders throughout this process: the Walters, the Aghilis, and, of course, the Thompsons. I appreciate you all!

To my second family, the Chus: Thank you for your endless support. I hope this book has made you proud!

My dad passed right after we finished the proposal for this book. I wish he were alive to see it now in its entirety, but I know I have gotten this far due to his unshakable faith in my writing and his love of food and travel that he passed down to me.

There are not enough words to thank my mom and my yai for gifting me with the Thai language and a love and curiosity of Thai food. Although I complained endlessly about attending Thai school in North Hollywood and La Puente every weekend growing up, I owe everything to those communities. My mom has answered a million questions about Thai food in all of my reporting and has always been relentlessly encouraging when it came to my dreams of being a writer. She is my favorite chef (sorry, Arnold!), and there is no me without her.

Finally, thank you to Jason: my life partner and my best friend. I am who I am because of your love, and I can do what I do due to your ceaseless support. You have seen me evolve through so many chapters of my own story, and I can't believe I get to realize this dream with you by my side.

- INDEX -

Note: Page numbers in *italics* indicate recipe photos.

Editor: Laura Dozier
Designer and Design Manager: Heesang Lee
Managing Editor: Krista Keplinger
Production Manager: Katie Gaffney

Library of Congress Control Number: 2025931135

ISBN: 978-1-4197-7638-0
eISBN: 979-8-88707-383-5

Le Murmure typeface created by Jérémy Landes (Velvetyne Type Foundry)

Printed and bound in China
10 9 8 7 6 5 4 3 2 1

ABRAMS The Art of Books
195 Broadway, New York, NY 10007
abramsbooks.com

This is my first cook book . . . it took me a long time to get it done. Our ***International Market & Restaurant*** *opened in 1975. We are the first Thai Foods in Nashville, Tennessee. We are very happy with our customers and our friends, who show a lot of kindness, and in return we always serve with friendliness and warm feelings.*

This cook book does not contain all the Thai dishes; there are more yet to come in future books.

Thank you to all my customers and all my family, who are behind all of my works and all the business.

This book is simple, and easy to follow. I hope you enjoy it. If you need help or if I can be of any assistance, please write or call me.

Patti K. Myint
International Market & Restaurant
2010 Belmont Blvd.
Nashville, Tennessee 37212
(615) 297-4453

Thank You!